A Beginners' Guide
to the
Dolls' House Hobby
REVISED AND EXPANDED EDITION

Jean Nisbett

Principal photography by Alec Nisbett

GUILD OF MASTER CRAFTSMAN PUBLICATIONS

Original edition of *A Beginners' Guide to the Dolls' House Hobby* first published 1997 by
Guild of Master Craftsman Publications Ltd.
166 High Street, Lewes
East Sussex, BN7 1XU

Reprinted 1997, 1998, 1999, 2000, 2001, 2002, 2003

This revised and expanded edition first published 2005

Text © Jean Nisbett 2005
Principal photography by Alec Nisbett

© in the work Guild of Master Craftsman Publications Ltd

ISBN 1 86108 486 2

British Cataloguing in Publication Data

A catalogue record of this book is available from the British Library.

Managing Editor: Gerrie Purcell
Production Manager: Hilary MacCallum
Editor: Alison Howard
Designer: Danny McBride

Colour reproduction by Altaimage Ltd.
Printed and bound by Sino Publishing House Ltd.

This book is for a new artistic generation,

Jay, Oliver, Martha, Millie, Bertie and Theo

with love.

Imperial and metric

The standard dolls' house scale is 1/12, which was based originally on imperial measures:
one inch represents one foot. Although many craftspeople use metric measurements, dolls' house
hobbyists in Britain and especially in America still use feet and inches. In this book imperial measures
of length are given first, followed by their metric equivalent. Accuracy to the millimetre is generally
unnecessary, and metric measurements may be rounded up or down a little.
Practically all the miniatures in this book are to 1/12 scale.

CONTENTS

PRACTICAL MATTERS

INTRODUCTION

There is something for everyone in the dolls' house hobby. It is a popular adult pastime in many countries, but children can also be involved. Dolls' houses appeal to people with a wide range of interests: the woodworker, the interior decorator, the artist and the needleworker can all find scope for their talents in this absorbing miniature world.

In the early 1980s the dolls' house hobby was just beginning to take off in Britain, although it was already well established in America. At that time I was happily restoring old dolls' houses I had found in junk shops and a local street market. I taught myself how to repair damaged woodwork, found out by trial and error which paints looked best on small-scale dwellings, and experimented with a variety of materials to make attractive flooring. Occasionally someone would bring

me a better class of house which they wanted me to decorate in period style. It was a short step from the renovation of old houses to the interior design and decoration of new, craftsman-made 1/12-scale dolls' houses. Still, nothing gives me a more pleasurable feeling of anticipation than a plain wooden house waiting to be transformed into a desirable residence.

Now that dolls' houses are so popular as a hobby for grown-ups, it is all much easier. Everything you could possibly want for your dolls' house is readily available

▼ A collector's dolls' house, arranged as a series of room sets rather than the more usual home. Six good-sized rooms and deep recesses in the front-opening doors allow plenty of space to display a variety of miniatures. A panel in the roof lifts off to reveal a loft.

in the internationally accepted 1/12 scale, including period-style wooden mouldings, doors and windows that can be assembled from kits, and flooring materials ranging from easy-to-cut sheets to individual Victorian tiles. These accessories can be mass-produced and inexpensive, or the sought-after work of specialist craftspeople.

If you are just starting out, this book will introduce you to the dolls' house hobby, showing a clear path through the confusion of choices. It will help you to decide what sort of dolls' house you really want; whether to make it from a kit or buy it ready-made and where to obtain everything you need.

Part One gives an overview of what is available and the decisions you need to make, while Part Two offers all the practical advice and information needed to make a start. I have included tried-and-tested

ideas for making furnishings and accessories, sometimes from the most surprising materials, plus suggestions for fixtures and fittings, with step-by-step instructions and easy-to-follow diagrams. Once you begin, you are sure to think of many new ideas.

Assembling furniture from kits is popular, and to help you achieve good results I have included some guidance which you may not find in the maker's instructions. The most charming dolls' houses generally contain a mixture of bought and home-made furnishings, just like a real home. Whether you decide to make or buy most of the contents, I am sure that you will enjoy every minute as you decorate and furnish a miniature home that will continue to delight you and your family for years to come. This book will help you to avoid expensive mistakes, save time trying to solve frustrating problems, and gain maximum enjoyment from a truly rewarding hobby.

◀ A desirable residence: a scale model of an early Victorian house.

1

Choosing your dolls' house

Before you buy your first dolls' house, think about what you want to achieve, and what will give you the greatest enjoyment. What is your main interest? It may be period-style decoration and furniture, collecting miniatures, making your own contents, design and decoration, or woodwork. Who is the house for? Many dolls' houses are equally suitable for a child or a collector, but if you are planning one specifically for a child your aims may be slightly different (see pages 50–56).

SCALE

The first thing you need to know is that most dolls' houses and their contents are made to a standard scale of 1/12. One inch represents 12 inches therefore, and 1cm represents 12cm. Although 12 is not a 'metric' number, these measurements are used internationally. Sample dimensions (opposite) should help you visualise how small everything will be. These measurements are the most common, but there will be some variation, particularly in the size of the rooms.

You may come across smaller scales: some dedicated craftspeople make 1/24 or even 1/48, but with the extra difficulties of decorating and furnishing in such a small size, these are more suitable for the devotee of the minuscule. For a first dolls' house it is best to choose the 1/12 scale, as it is much easier to find wallpaper, furniture and accessories.

▶ This appealing Georgian house takes up little space as it is smaller than the more usual 1/12 scale. Most of the contents were made specially to fit the tiny rooms.

Sample dimensions

ROOMS		Dining chair	1½in (40mm) to seat
Depth	9½–10½in (240–270mm)		3in (75mm) high
Ceiling height	9–11in (225–275mm)	Wardrobe	6½in (165mm) high
Width of room	9½–10½in (240–270mm)	Armchair/sofa	1½in (40mm) to seat
			(height to back varies)
FURNITURE		Dining table	2½in (65mm) high
Four-poster bed	6½in (165mm) high		(length and width vary)
	6in (150mm) long	**DOLLS**	
	5in (130mm) wide	Man	6in (150mm) tall
Single bed	6in (150mm) long	Woman	5½in (140mm) tall
	3in (75mm) wide	Child	3–4in (75–100mm) tall
Double bed	5in (130mm) wide	Toddler	2½–3in (65–75mm) tall

ADVANCE PLANNING

There is so much choice that it is wise to do some advance planning before you buy. You probably know roughly how much you can spend on a house and are likely to be able to spend on your hobby in future. Whether it is a large or small amount, you still need to work out your priorities. If money is no object, a house can be commissioned from one of the craftspeople who make to order, fully decorated both inside and out. For most of us, what we can afford is likely to be much closer to what a drama enthusiast might spend on theatre tickets, or a film buff on visits to the cinema.

Enjoyment of the hobby is certainly not dependent on how much you spend. Miniature interior design and decoration is something anyone can learn. Making furniture, or assembling it from kits, is rewarding in itself and you will find that you can make many attractive accessories and ornaments from inexpensive materials. It is wise to decide first what size house would suit you best. For a beginner on a limited budget, a two- or four-room house is a good way to gain experience before going on to something larger. A nine-room house will cost a lot to furnish, even if you make many of the items yourself, but is an ideal long-term project. Consider how much time you have. Making everything yourself, whether from bits and pieces or from kits, is time-consuming but very satisfying, and collecting gives you an excuse for trips to miniatures fairs and dolls' house shops. Whichever approach appeals, your house will evolve gradually.

PRICES AND QUALITY

An inexpensive house will have a basic staircase without balusters or handrail, and the rooms will be empty boxes. A more expensive model may be fitted with chimney breasts and even interior doors. You will need to balance the amount of money available and the amount of work you want to do yourself.

Most moderately-priced, ready-made dolls' houses are supplied undecorated. There are wide variations in price, even between houses which at first glance seem similar. In general, this reflects not only the detailing but also the material used, and in most cases this will be either MDF (medium density fibreboard) or plywood. MDF is less expensive than plywood, and has a smooth surface that takes a paint finish well. It is heavier, which can be a disadvantage if you want to move a large house around. Plywood can split if it is of poor quality, especially when screws are used to assemble the house, and may warp if it is placed too near a radiator. Nonetheless, it is essential if you plan to create an antique effect and want to stain and polish, or varnish, the façade of your house.

It should be easy to find your nearest dolls' house shop in the telephone directory, and miniatures fairs in your area will be advertised in the local press. Visiting one will give you a clear idea of the options available.

▲ In the 18th and early 19th centuries, Gothic style was favoured for cottages on English country estates. This ready-built, two-room version has an attractive, unusual façade, and is a good starter home. A spiral staircase fits neatly into a corner, leaving plenty of space for furniture.

▶ A well-made plywood house with printed black lettering on the façade was finished using satin varnish. It took eight coats to produce a perfect result, but was well worth the effort. Coloured satin varnish was used for the door.

Even if you spend very little, you should come home full of ideas and inspiration. Dolls' house hobby magazines are the most practical way to discover suitable stockists, and where to contact makers. They contain helpful and practical features and pictures as well as listing forthcoming miniatures fairs that may not be too far away. There will also be addresses for dolls' house shops and mail order suppliers which will be able to provide the items mentioned in this book, as well as details of miniatures that are made by specialist craftspeople.

HOUSES MADE FROM KITS

A dolls' house to build from a kit will cost around half to two-thirds of the price of the same model ready-made, depending on the complexity of the design. MDF kits have ready-cut slots and grooves to be fitted together and glued, which makes them easy to assemble and ideal for the beginner. If you have some model-making or woodwork experience, you will probably be able to tackle a plywood kit house. This requires more work and involves screws as well as glue in the assembly. You will also need to use some woodworking tools (see page 59).

ROOM BOXES

If space and money for your new hobby is very limited, you can create your first miniature scene in a room box. It is surprising how much can be achieved. Room boxes are available either furnished or as kits to assemble yourself, and some have a sliding acrylic front to keep out dust. An average size of 15in wide x 10in high x 9in deep (380 x 255 x 230mm) gives plenty of space. Alternatively, you could use a suitably-sized wooden box, and I have even seen miniature scenes created in an old clock case.

▶ A terrace house built from a kit has all the charm of its Victorian original. It is 16in wide x 16½in deep x 29½in high (410 x 420 x 750mm). The bonus with this design is that it can be supplied with a shop front at no extra cost.

BUILDING FROM A KIT

Many newcomers to the dolls' house hobby will prefer to buy a ready-made house and concentrate on the decoration and furnishings. If you have decided to take on the challenge (and financial saving) of constructing your own house, however, here are some practical tips to supplement the instructions provided by the manufacturer:

1 Check first that all the parts are included in the kit. Lay them out and familiarize yourself with them.

2 Read the instructions provided carefully, checking the parts mentioned in each stage of assembly and making sure that you understand how they fit together.

3 Sand each piece until it is smooth using fine glasspaper, grade 0 or 00.

4 Check that any pre-cut grooves are the right size to take slot-in parts. You may need to make minute adjustments by sanding to ensure a perfect fit.

5 Assemble each stage 'dry' and check that all is correct before you use wood glue. Once the glue has set it will be impossible to undo.

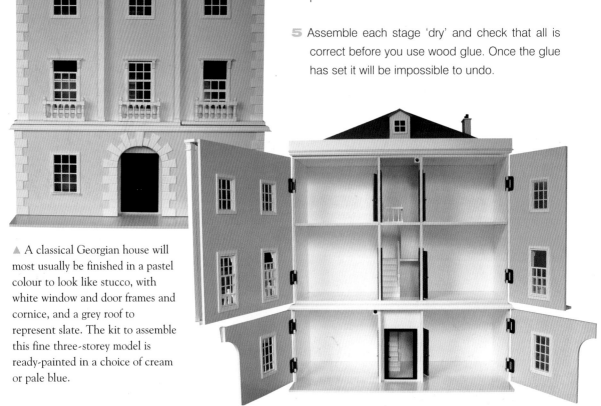

▲ A classical Georgian house will most usually be finished in a pastel colour to look like stucco, with white window and door frames and cornice, and a grey roof to represent slate. The kit to assemble this fine three-storey model is ready-painted in a choice of cream or pale blue.

▲ The inside is also ready-painted, and is completed with a central staircase.

6 While the glue is setting, it is best to hold the pieces firmly together with masking tape, as it will take several hours until full strength is achieved.

7 Ensure that walls and floors are at right angles, or you could end up with a leaning house. Check every angle with a set square and if necessary improvise a jig using blocks of wood with perfectly squared corners, or even piles of books. Use the jig to support the structure while the glue dries.

8 If a staircase is provided, but is not designed to be built in during the initial assembly, it is far more practical not to glue it in place until you have decorated the rooms.

Once constructed, your kit house will be at the same stage as an undecorated, ready-made model, waiting for the first steps in the decorative processes that will turn the shell of a house into something bright, expressive and personal.

▲ This fine Victorian house can be built from a kit, or supplied ready-assembled and with lighting. All the period architectural details have been faithfully reproduced. Tackling a kit for a large house is not necessarily more difficult than a small one – it just takes longer.

EXTENSIONS

Apart from price considerations, one advantage of building a house from a kit is that you can start small and extend later. Several makers supply additional basement kits that will provide two or three extra rooms and an attractive front area with entrance steps and railings. A ready-built house can sometimes be enlarged by adding a complete extra wing.

◀ Another good choice for a beginner, Willow Cottage has a charming appearance with plenty of realistic detail. It is available as an easy-to-assemble MDF kit, and the basement is an additional, separate kit.

2
Period properties

Many dolls' houses are made in period styles and often a fascination with a particular era draws people into the hobby. Georgian style is always popular, with Tudor and Victorian not far behind. Craftspeople make more miniature furniture from these periods because of the demand, but other styles are catching up rapidly, especially Edwardian, the 1930s and the 1940s. Deciding on your favourite may be easy but choosing a dolls' house is a little like buying a real one: you know it is right when you see it. Plans you have made for a country cottage or a Georgian town house may be forgotten when you fall in love with a three-bedroomed semi or a Gothic folly.

The exterior of the house is usually the deciding factor in your choice, but it is also important to inspect the inside thoroughly. Does the internal layout suit your ideas? Ease of access is vital: whatever the style of house it will be simpler to paint and decorate if, for example, the window glazing is not fixed in first. Removable staircases are also convenient for the dolls' house decorator; some makers fix them with slots, or an easily removable screw (see page 100 for advice on decorating around staircases).

◀ The semi-detached house from between the first and second World Wars has a nostalgic charm which appeals to many people, and is already a period piece. This well-designed example can be supplied ready-made or built from a kit or plans.

PERIOD STYLE

Once you have chosen, decide how you want the completed house to look before you begin on the decoration. It is easy to re-paper or repaint the rooms inside if you change your mind, but it is far more difficult to redecorate the outside successfully. The types of finish used for the exterior are tricky to remove and you may not get a perfectly smooth finish if you redecorate, especially if the architectural features of the house have also been altered.

The exterior finish can be simple or elaborate, but the effect will be better if colours and materials are suited to the period style of the house. If possible, study some actual examples. Look at magazines that specialise in the restoration of period buildings for examples of authentic paint colours, or to see how a particular house might have looked in its heyday. Even with a modern dolls' house, it is worth doing research to gain ideas for colour schemes.

▶ Silver Jubilee House, shown in its undecorated state on page 15, has been transformed with a brick and stucco front and a slate roof.

DEGREES OF DETAIL

There are many finishes you can use on the outside of your dolls' house, depending on how much you like messing about with paint and glue. I find great satisfaction in mixing paint colours and achieving the perfect shade I have in mind for a particular house. For a realistic special effect, plaster, stucco or pebbledash can be simulated (see page 67). The roof can be simply painted, papered to resemble roof tiles or slates or, if you want to be more adventurous, you can add wooden shingles or realistic-looking ceramic tiles (see page 73).

On a dolls' house with exterior walls painted or resembling brick, window frames look best painted off-white for an attractive contrast, rather than the darker colour wood that might have been used on an actual house.

If your main interest is interior furnishings or collecting miniatures, there is no need for what might seem like hard work on the exterior. A simple, painted finish in well-chosen colours on the walls and roof should be ideal. The simple guide on pages 20–22 will help you to decide what finishes will fit your needs and type of house. Practical information on how to achieve specific effects are given in Part Two (see pages 66–68).

▲ The porch is a particularly attractive feature and the well-chosen paint colours make the entrance look welcoming.

ARCHITECTURAL DETAIL

A dolls' house can have architectural details so accurate that it is almost a model of a real one, and you can decide how far you wish to go. The hallmark of the Victorian town house, painted stucco, is easily copied in a paint finish. In the interests of accuracy, you might want to add Tuscan columns to support a portico, lintels above the windows, or perhaps pediments and architrave on the façade. Wooden bargeboards or shutters can add charm to a simple, country-style house, and quoining will enhance a plain brick one (see page 76). These details are readily obtainable as reasonably-priced 1/12-scale plaster or cast resin mouldings which can be painted and attached with glue.

▶ A scaled-down replica of an early Victorian house from the 1830s. These houses followed the standard Georgian plan inside, without the over-elaboration which characterised later Victorian style. The balcony and the railings are fine examples of miniaturised wrought-iron work.

◀ Victoria House is based on a typical 19th-century house on the Isle of Anglesey. It is available ready-made, but for the woodworker all the parts can be supplied separately. There are six rooms, with two rear windows to let in extra light.

▶ The house is transformed by an attractive colour scheme, with stone paint, a slate roof and brightly coloured front door.

DECORATION

If you want to paint the exterior of your dolls' house in authentic period colour, all the help you need is at hand. Many paint manufacturers have researched this area and can provide useful shade cards in a range of historic paint colours.

One or two paint sample pots will be sufficient to decorate a dolls' house. Even if samples are not available you should still be able to obtain a small amount of specially-mixed paint. Some special colours are made only in oil-based paints or to an old-fashioned distemper formula which is more difficult to work with. To avoid this, it is generally best to choose something as near as possible to your ideal from a modern range of paints. Look carefully at the shade card when choosing stains and varnishes. Sometimes it is better to settle for a shade that you can see is what you want, rather than be guided by the name of the finish the product is supposed to represent. On a small scale, it will be equally effective. The following table is a brief guide to colours and finishes commonly used in particular eras.

Period	Finishes
TUDOR/JACOBEAN (16th/early 17th century)	
Walls	Plaster with half-timbering; white, ochre, pale pink or apricot infilling
Timbers	Use walnut stain, which is warmer than light oak, to complement pale-coloured plaster*
Windows and doors	Wood stain or varnish doors and window surrounds to match
Roof	Stone tiles or simulated thatch
	Blackened timbers were a Victorian fashion and look striking with white plaster
GEORGIAN (18th century)	
Walls	Painted as stucco for a town house, in stone-coloured paint; a small Georgian cottage might be pink, pale blue or cream
Roof	Grey or russet slates, or paint
Windows	Pure white or 'Georgian' white (off-white) for frames and surrounds
Front door	Dark green, black or white
Railings	Georgian houses today usually have black-painted railings, but a dark bronze-green is more authentic

REGENCY (early 19th century)

Walls	Stucco: painted finish in pale green, pale yellow or apricot, with details picked out in white
Roof	Grey slates, or grey paint
Front door	Dark green
Additions	Wedgwood plaques or plaster friezes; Greek key design frieze below cornice

VICTORIAN TOWN HOUSE (19th century)

Walls	Brick (use printed paper, or plasticized sheets – see page 72
Roof	Grey slate, or grey paint
Front door	Black or deep blue
Additions	Brass door furniture and letter box

* London stock brick was pale yellow. In other areas, bricks made from local clay might have been red or dark purple-grey

VICTORIAN COUNTRY HOUSE (19th century)

Walls	Red brick
Roof	Slate grey
Front door	Dark green
Additions	Bargeboards on gable ends; a clock tower or roof turret

EDWARDIAN (early 20th century)

Walls	Brick
Roof	Red slates, or paint (russet mix)
Paintwork	White
Front door	Stained as oak; stained glass panels
Additions	Balcony or verandah, painted white Mock half-timbers on gable end

1930s–1940s

Walls	Brick or pebble dash
Roof	Red or grey slates
Paintwork	Mid-green
Front door	Mid-green, white or stained as oak
Additions	Letter box; stained glass panel over front door; porch, tiled red

FARMHOUSE

Walls	'Sussex' pink, ochre, or white
Roof	Slate, or stone tiles
Paintwork	White, or oak timber
Front door	Stained oak or white

18TH-CENTURY SHAKER OR ENGLISH CLAPBOARD HOUSE

Weatherboard (UK)	Stained dark with woodstain
Siding (US)	Painted white

CHOOSING THE DECOR

When you have made some decisions about the outside of your house, you can turn your attention to the inside and let your imagination run free. First, decide whether it is to have period or modern room settings. Up-to-date interiors are perfectly acceptable in a period house, or you may prefer everything to be in keeping with the style of the house. Alternatively, modern room settings mean that you can achieve an agreeable mix of antique furniture and modern items. When you have chosen the style of the rooms, you can start to think about colour. Remember that when you look into the house you will see all the rooms at once. It makes sense to coordinate your schemes to some extent, to avoid clashing colours in adjacent rooms. Strive for a happy medium: an all-pastel arrangement might look insipid, while very strong colours will be too dominant. Off-white ceilings look best in a dolls' house of any period, as they reflect soft light into the room.

The table opposite lists appropriate colours and styles for period interiors, but there is always scope for imagination and alternatives. More specific room details can also be found in the table.

Period	Finishes
TUDOR/JACOBEAN (16th/early 17th century)	
Walls	Colour-washed in ochre, white or terracotta, or oak panelling (light or dark)
Ceilings	Oak beams (light or dark), which can be stained or painted in a decorative pattern of red, green and gold
Floors	Flagstones or oak planking
Features	Large open fireplace made of stone or brick, or plastered; logs arranged in an iron basket or on firedogs; planked doors and stencilled decoration; inglenook fireplace (for a cottage)
GEORGIAN (18th century)	
Walls	Paint in a limited palette of colours: stone, drab and mouse (a sort of fawn or grey); pea green or pearl for the best rooms
Wainscoting	Painted panelling below the dado rail
Doors	Often painted dark brown or deep red
LATE GEORGIAN (1780-1810)	
Walls	Robert Adam-style colours: pink, green, blue and white paint, highlighted with gold for a grand effect, or wallpaper (including flock)
Ceilings	White
Floors	Planking, not highly polished
Additions	Plaster cornices; deep skirtings; pediments over doors
Details	Dado rail; Adam-style fireplace for grand rooms; simple hob grate for a small house; six-panelled doors

REGENCY (early 19th century)

Walls	Wallpaper, or Chinese-style decoration
Ceilings	White
Floors	Planking, as before
Features	Elaborately draped curtains; striped fabrics (bright acid yellow was very popular) or simple white muslin; gilded mirrors and candles in wall sconces

EARLY VICTORIAN (1837–1870)   A light and pretty style which gradually became darker and heavier; fitted carpet became standard

LATE VICTORIAN (1870–1901)

Ceilings	White.
Features	Elaborate fireplaces, in marble or faux marble; curtains in velvet or heavy silk with inner lace curtains, and blinds
Additions	Footstools, occasional tables, workboxes, firescreens, draped tables (see page 112), four-panelled doors

WILLIAM MORRIS STYLE (late 19th century)

Walls	William Morris wallpaper is available in 1/12 scale, or use giftwrap based on William Morris designs, which were inspired by medieval ideas
Curtains	Liberty dress fabrics in William Morris designs
Ceilings	White
Paintwork	White
Flooring	Planked, light oak
Additions	Plate rack or picture rail; carpets in oriental or William Morris designs

RENNIE MACKINTOSH STYLE (early 20th century)

Walls	White
Ceilings	White
Flooring	Plain, pale carpeting
Paintwork	White; occasionally very dark, almost black, but white looks better in dolls' houses
Features	Gesso (plaster) wall plaques (see page 41); high-backed chairs; stained glass where possible (light fittings, door panels); stencilled motifs in stylised rose design

EDWARDIAN (early 20th century)

Walls	Patterned wallpapers (often floral), borders, panelling and deep friezes were all popular; a picture rail with a border below or a frieze above was often used (see page 106)
Flooring	Polished wooden floor or linoleum surround, with carpet square
Paintwork	White or stained medium oak
Additions	Mirror above fireplace; stained glass panels in front door; grate with tiled surround and elaborate mantelshelf, sometimes incorporating shelves on either side

1930s–1940s

Kitchens	Green and cream were standard, with half-tiled walls; quarry-tiled floor
Bedrooms	Often pink
Lounge	Cream-washed walls with green, fawn or floral soft furnishings or, for the wealthy, a room entirely in shades of white and cream
Floors	Carpet square (patterned) with wood-grained floor surround in medium oak
Accessories	Standard lamps; hearthrug; companion set (poker, tongs and hearthbrush on a brass stand); Art Deco-style wall lights/bronze statuettes; silk or velvet cushions; flying ducks on the wall
Paintwork	Cream or wood-grain finish

3
Planning the interior

After you have decided what period your house will be, whether an older style or something more up-to-date, decide which rooms you would like to include. Space is at a premium in a small dolls' house, but if you have more than three rooms at your disposal you can go beyond the usual living room, kitchen and bedroom which will probably appear in one form or another, whatever the period of your house. This is your chance to be an interior designer, without the constraints imposed by a real house, in which certain rooms such as the kitchen and bathroom may have to be plumbed for water or tiled, and are not so easily interchangeable. With a dolls' house, you can choose a large kitchen and a small, cosy living room or vice versa, depending how you visualise your completed house, and what types of furniture and decoration appeal to you.

DESIGN CONSIDERATIONS

If you want to create a complete period dolls' house, the architectural style can be carried through to the design and arrangement of the room. A modern interior is more flexible, even in a house with a period exterior, because you can decide exactly how much has been 'updated'. You might, for example, want to site a radiator on one of the walls rather than have an open fireplace. Be cautious about mixing too many styles of period furniture with modern. Choose a few pieces of Tudor, Regency or Victorian, depending on preference, but try to keep to one additional period style, or the result will look messy. To give an idea of what is involved in the interior decoration of a whole house, specific suggestions for a variety of rooms follow. You may wish to refer to the interior decoration table (see pages 22–25). Practical instructions for some of the main items are in Part Two.

▶ Dolls busy with their various occupations give this interior an actively lived-in feeling.

THE ENTRANCE HALL

Make the most of the entrance hall, whatever its size. It is amazing what you can do with a space only about 3 x 5in (75 x 125mm), and a large square hall can look magnificent. Even if it is tiny, the entrance hall sets the tone of the house so it is worth taking some trouble over it.

In a Victorian house, you might fit in an umbrella stand; in an Edwardian house there could be a hall stand for hanging hats and coats. Hang a picture or mirror on the wall; put a doormat or rug on the floor, and you instantly achieve a lived-in feel. If you have a front porch, it could be tiled with reproduction Victorian or Art Nouveau tiles, or black and white tiles

in a checkerboard pattern. Use either real ceramic tiles or pieces of plasticized card, which is thinner and, unlike ceramic tiles, will not usually cause problems when opening the front door (see page 96 for advice on adjusting the front door if necessary).

▼ I divided the ground floor of my early Victorian house to make an impressive hall, an unusual feature in a dolls' house. In this period the drawing room was usually on the first floor, so a reception hall is appropriate. Though I generally prefer my houses unpopulated, the hall is often a scene of bustling activity, and I arranged it to include both adult and child dolls.

KITCHENS

For many people their favourite dolls' house room is the kitchen, especially if it is in an older style. Now that we have microwave ovens that work at the touch of a switch and much of the guesswork has been taken out of cooking, we seem all the more fascinated by how things were done in the past. We may not actually want to go back to those days, but it can be great fun to recreate old-fashioned kitchens in 1/12 scale.

▼ This Victorian kitchen is one of my favourite rooms. There is always enough space left to fit in one more culinary treat or kitchen gadget.

TUDOR OR JACOBEAN

All cooking was done over an open fire, so an inglenook is essential. An inglenook is a large, open fireplace and the top is formed by the insertion of a long, heavy beam. A 1/12-scale version is simple to construct (see page 97) and it should be made first, before you decorate, as it can take up a whole wall. Cooking utensils in those days were rudimentary. There would have been a metal rod over the fire, with a cauldron or two suspended from hooks (see page 84 for instructions on how to make a realistic-looking fire). Joints of meat or game could be hung from the ceiling, and there should be a cupboard for bread. Washing-up arrangements are not a problem in the Tudor dolls' house: the pump was outside and plates were simply wiped clean after use.

GEORGIAN AND REGENCY

Georgian kitchens also had few aids for the cook. All water still had to be brought in from outside, so each kitchen would have had a bucket. Food needed to be kept out of the reach of mice, so shelves and high cupboards are essential. To add a busy, lived-in look, the kitchen can be festooned with ladles, spoons, blackened saucepans, a kettle suspended over the fire and a jack to turn the spit for cooking meat.

VICTORIAN

The Victorian kitchen seems to be the most popular with dolls' house enthusiasts. So many tiny items can be included – cooking utensils and gadgets, copper saucepans, food both fresh and cooked, baskets of vegetables, bowls, jugs and basins. As much as

▲ A Cotswold-style oak dresser shows off an eye-catching dinner service in a traditional willow pattern-design as well as a set of mugs.

possible can be crammed in to good effect; the only limit is the amount of space you have available. At the last count, there were 145 items in my Victorian kitchen, which is one of my favourite rooms (see photograph opposite).

The 19th century saw the beginnings of modern plumbing, so the Victorian kitchen can include a ceramic Belfast sink and a wooden draining board, perhaps with a wooden plate rack above.

The range is a vital focal point and can be built in very easily (see page 94), with space at the side for a coal scuttle, and a wide mantelshelf for ornaments. You will probably want to include a dresser, so that the shelves can be filled with crockery and other utensils.

▲ The range in this late Victorian kitchen is set in a tiled surround. The patterned tiles are replicas of the work of 19th-century designer William De Morgan, interspersed with plain green tiles.

◀ A gourmet's delight: these elaborate tiered arrangements are worthy of Mrs Beeton and would make a superb centrepiece for the Georgian or Victorian table.

You should give some thought to the room layout, because both the range and the dresser look best viewed from the front. Unless your kitchen has one long wall at the back, one or other is going to have to fit against a side wall. I have arranged dolls' house kitchens in both ways and think that, in general, the range looks best on the back wall. If you then place the dresser fairly near to the front of the house on a side wall, you will find that its well-filled shelves can be clearly seen.

Most dolls' house kitchens are small, and are likely to be deep and relatively narrow. The proportions of the room are improved if the range is set against the back wall and a chimney breast the full width of the kitchen is brought forward about 1½in (40mm) from the back wall. The space behind this new upper section of wall is an open chimney above the range. The same method applies when constructing an inglenook fireplace.

▼ This large four-oven Aga will look impressive if your kitchen is spacious enough to take it. It is offered complete, in a choice of authentic Aga colours. Smaller models with two ovens and models in earlier styles are also available.

1930s–1940s

Kitchens changed radically in the late 1920s and early 1930s, with the beginning of the servantless society. For many wealthy ladies this was the first time they had to think about cooking and it is surprising how much more convenient kitchens became. Vogue magazine even published articles on how to make sandwiches and prepare simple meals, which may seem amusing now, but for those with no culinary experience it must have been extremely helpful.

The Aga cooker arrived on the scene in 1929 and almost immediately became the status symbol it still is. You might like to fit one into your early 20th-century kitchen, either a ready-made model or one you have constructed yourself (see page 122). The fitted kitchen was not common in the UK. Most kitchens were furnished with a cabinet based on a bureau, with a closed cupboard at the bottom and a glass-fronted top so that china, usually with a decorative floral pattern, could be seen. A pull-down flap at table height provided an extra work surface on which plates could be laid out.

There might also be a small rectangular table with two fold-down flaps to save space. Quarry tiles or linoleum on the floor could be washed easily. Kitchens were often tiled to half-way up the wall, as this was thought hygienic. Refrigerators were not common and most food would be stored in a larder leading off the kitchen. In the dolls' house, this could be simplified by storing food on shelves in the kitchen itself.

▼ In this well-used 1930s kitchen with its evidence of recent baking, baskets of groceries and fruit have been delivered by the grocer's boy. Tea towels have been hung to air over the Aga, on a rack that is worked by pulleys.

LIVING ROOMS

The name for the room where the family would sit and relax has changed over the centuries. The solar, the withdrawing room, the parlour, the drawing room, the lounge and the sitting room all mean much the same thing, but there are definite distinctions of style, depending on what degree of formality or informality was expected at the time.

▼ Plain white walls are the perfect background for blackened beams. The fireplaces of this Tudor house are of cast resin which needs no painting to resemble stone. A log basket is essential.

▲ An effective way to display a small collection of wind instruments is to attach them to the wall using adhesive putty. Be careful when fixing: it is all too easy to snap a slender wooden recorder in half by applying pressure at the wrong point.

TUDOR OR JACOBEAN HALL AND SOLAR

The Tudor house was dominated by the hall, a large room where everyone ate and slept. The centrepiece was usually an oak refectory table with benches on either side and a chair at the head. The walls might be hung with tapestries or decorated with stencilling (see page 106), and a log fire in the large fireplace would make the room look inviting.

The solar was a private room where the master of the house and his family could retreat from the hustle and bustle of a large household. Furniture was sparse but could include several rectangular wooden stools known as 'joint stools' because of the method of construction, sometimes decorated with carving, and a wooden armchair for the master of the house. This would also have carved decoration, particularly on the back. An oak side table could hold pewter mugs and a flagon, or wooden plates or bowls. Floors were uncovered, but a prized carpet was sometimes used as a table covering to add a rich effect as carpets were far too valuable to walk on. The lady of the house would probably have an embroidery frame to work on. Music was a popular home entertainment and the Tudor solar can be brought to life by including some instruments.

QUEEN ANNE PARLOUR

During the reign of Queen Anne (1702–14) furniture styles changed to become more comfortable. The winged armchair was designed to protect its occupant from draughts and is still popular today. Panelled rooms were still much in use, with white-painted or walnut panelling. Lighting could come from girandoles (wall lights) – candle brackets backed by small mirrors to reflect the light.

▲ A cosy Queen Anne parlour, complete with winged armchair and fine wooden furniture.

GEORGIAN DRAWING ROOM

As the 18th century progressed manners became more formal. In leisure moments, the family probably retreated to a small parlour, but the drawing room, used for entertaining guests, tended to be severe and elegant. This is the ideal room to display a collection of fine miniatures, but bear in mind that the formality of the time extended to the arrangement of furniture. Chairs were placed at intervals around the walls, and a dado rail was usually added to stop chair backs from marking the paint or wallpaper (see page 92).

◀ Symmetry was much admired and ornaments were displayed in pairs if possible. Pictures were hung higher than is customary today. A pole firescreen was obligatory, as it could be moved easily to protect the complexions of those sitting near the fire.

◀ A Regency drawing room arranged for music. The chaise longue allows the hostess to relax while listening to the evening's entertainment. The panels with musical motifs are cut from a sheet of 1/12 wallpaper and arranged to suit the room.

REGENCY DRAWING ROOM

Life during the Regency period in England (1811–20) was fairly boisterous and, in contrast to the severity of the previous decades, it became customary to arrange the seating in an informal manner. Little tables were set ready to play cards and to hold drinking glasses, and comfortable sofas were placed near the fire. Decoration in grander houses was ostentatious and this is a period where you can add gilded cornices and elaborate ornaments without overdoing things. A drawing room in such a house would be completed with mirrors and candelabra.

VICTORIAN PARLOUR

Early Victorian style was a simpler version of Regency elegance, but later in the 19th century, clutter abounded. A Victorian parlour, especially one of the period around 1880 can be great fun to put together. The more ornaments the better, with rows of pictures in gilded frames hung on the walls (see opposite). Workboxes and footstools can be scattered about. Windows can be adorned with velvet or silk curtains edged with braid or bobble fringe, plus inner curtains of net or lace. Blinds could be used in some rooms. Carpets add an air of comfort. These can be of needlepoint or cross stitch, and you can make them yourself, either from one of the many small-scale kits or charts available, or by adapting a specific pattern from a full-size design. Fitted carpets were becoming popular at this time, and one idea pioneered by Queen Victoria was plaid carpet. This is easy to reproduce using wool tartan dress material, and can look very effective. The best way to lay fitted carpet is with double-sided tape, so you can take it up easily when you feel it is time for a change.

◀ A modern sitting room furnished with 'antiques' and a large, comfortable-looking sofa. The trompe l'oeil patio (a picture cut from a magazine), partly screened by lavishly-draped curtains, provides an outside view.

ROOMS FOR MODERN LIVING

For an up-to-date sitting room you might like to go for the 'country house' style that is so popular with professional interior decorators. Be lavish with fabric, which for miniature settings is inexpensive. For curtains and cushions use dress material with small prints, or Indian silks which are thin enough to hang well. Cover sofas and armchairs with floral print fabric. The trick when making a dolls' house cushion is to be economical with the stuffing. A small twist of polyester wadding is sufficient, as you want it to look squashy and comfortable. To furnish the room, easy chairs or armless sofas are simple to make from scratch (see pages 108–110). Do not worry if your seams are not perfect: simply cover them by glueing or sewing on thin braid. A round table with a floor-length cloth could hold ornaments and photographs in silver frames. Vases of flowers will add to the fresh and luxurious look of the room.

▼ This comfortable parlour is an example of the time when High Victorian style was beginning to give way to newer styles including a passion for tartan. Home and family were very important and a range of family activities is catered for.

DINING ROOM

The eating room, as it used to be called, has altered little in its basic arrangements over the years; it is only the decorations that change. Whatever the period, you will need a dining table and chairs (or benches) and some sort of sideboard – a plain oak trestle table for a Tudor room, or a bow-fronted mahogany sideboard for a Georgian room. A Georgian dining room should have a mahogany table, which can be set with a miniature dinner service, including glasses and perhaps a centrepiece of fruit in a glass or silver container. In a Victorian dining room a round table can be covered with a floor-length cloth (see page 112).

▼ A lacy cloth will conceal a plain table and set off a display of food.

▲ This exquisitely-painted service is laid on a table from a set of children's dolls' house furniture, showing that it is possble to mix craftsman-made miniatures with ordinary ones to good effect.

MAKING FOOD

Food is, of course, the most important thing in a dining room. A table laid with a meal ready to eat always looks enticing. Professional miniaturists make delicious-looking replicas of a wide variety of food, but you can make your own using a modelling compound. These are available in many colours and are hardened in the oven to make them permanent. Follow the instructions given and you will be surprised how easy it is. With a little practice you will be able to make food fit for a banquet. If you enjoy painting and are happy to spend a bit more time, it is more economical to use natural-coloured modelling compound and then paint the pieces yourself.

BEDROOMS

Throughout history the bedroom seems to have been considered the woman's domain. Even if the rest of your dolls' house is quite plain, you might indulge in a spot of luxury for the main bedroom. Pretty floral prints, a draped dressing table (see page 113), curtains with tiebacks, and a lace or patchwork bedspread all look delightful in miniature form.

▲ This bed was copied from a similar version in an early Heal's catalogue. The comfortable-looking sprung mattress was specially made to fit the bed.

▲ A white-painted metal bedstead with brass knobs would look well in an Edwardian bedroom: the lacy coverlet and satin eiderdown are typical of the time. The needlepoint rug was worked from half of a design intended as a needlecase.

A bed is the easiest piece of furniture to make yourself using a small box as a base, which will be covered by the bedding. There is also a wonderful choice of ready-made 'antique' beds, which can be expensive, depending on the craftsmanship involved. You may like to start off with a home-made bed while you save up for a real showpiece. Keep the size of the bedroom in mind, because while a double bed or a four-poster may be impressive, it will probably take up too much space in a small room (see page 11 for a size guide). It is sometimes wiser to choose a single bed for a modern room setting, or a half-tester rather than a four-poster bed.

◀ Patchwork quilts always attract admiration. If your construction time is limited, one easy option is to use a quilt made from printed fabric with a finely detailed design that mimics the real thing effectively.

BATHROOM

Bathrooms only became standard features in UK houses in the 1930s. Until then it was usual to have a jug and basin on a marble-topped washstand in the bedroom. If your house is more modern, a bathroom can look splendid, whether it is in clean white or something rather more elaborate. Brass taps and 'glass' shelves made of clear acrylic will add sparkle, and it is now possible to find 1/12 scale versions of everything from toothbrushes to soap.

▶ Bathrooms as we now know them were unheard of in the late 18th and early 19th centuries, but in some stately homes the owner had a marble plunge bath (cold water only), often in a specially built marble bath house. Other inventive ideas were occasionally tried, like this Regency shower, which needed the aid of a servant to pump the water and to empty it.

◀ Bathrooms became a feature of the larger home during the early 20th century, though there was generally only one to serve several bedrooms. A deep washbasin set into a marble-topped cupboard, brass taps, an elegant chair and large white fluffy towels were typical, and are still found in many country houses today.

▲ Corner baths fitted with opulent gold-plated taps came into fashion during the 1970s. Thick, fluffy carpet (known as shag pile) also began to be used in bathrooms.

▲ A shower takes up little space in a modern dolls' house. Wall tiles can be bought in sheet form to avoid the chore of glueing on individual tiles, and plastic-coated tile paper can look good on a floor.

NURSERY

Planning a nursery is fun and exciting in real life, and in a dolls' house it can give continued enjoyment. My Victorian nursery contains far more toys than would have been provided in reality, and has developed over many years.

The Victorian period is particularly rich in fascinating toys. Some of the 1/12-scale models are so tiny that they have to be made in metal for precision and durability. They also have moving parts and can be played with just like their full-size counterparts. Such items are a delight to seek out and collect, and are likely to catch the eye of any visitor.

You might also consider including child dolls in a nursery. Even if you have no visible inhabitants in the rest of the house, dolls in the nursery make the whole scene come to life, especially if you have a rocking horse to set in motion.

▲ Whether Victorian or modern, a nursery can be one of the most interesting rooms to arrange. The toys in this one have been collected over many years.

UNUSUAL ROOMS

The rooms mentioned so far would be found in the average home, but it is always an interesting challenge for the miniaturist to create a room setting which is out of the ordinary. If your house is large enough, or you are planning another dolls' house, or even if you are keen to include an unusual room in a small house, you might enjoy one of these ideas.

18TH-CENTURY PRINT ROOM

Print rooms became popular in Regency times, and were often created by the ladies of the household, who would cut out and paste up original prints to decorate the walls. The pictures were lithographs, usually of views, classical subjects or portraits of eminent people. A few print rooms still exist. I was so impressed with the arrangement at Stratfield Saye, the former country home of the Duke of Wellington, that I decided to try some cutting and pasting myself. I used a miniaturized sheet of print room designs to decorate the card room shown in the photograph. Prints cut from magazines are an alternative, and it is worth keeping an eye out for suitable articles.

It is not necessary to fill all the walls of the room, which might be a little oppressive, especially on a small scale. For maximum effect, simply make an arrangement over the fireplace, round a door, or in a group over a side table. A border design alone can also be effective. Even if you have no room that you can dedicate as a print room, you could consider displaying prints in the hall and up the stairwell.

▲ Walls decorated with prints in 18th-century fashion make the perfect setting for this Regency card room. Packs of miniature playing cards are inexpensive but difficult to keep tidy. I used only a few cards from a pack and arranged them as though in play, secured with dabs of adhesive putty. The George III-style round table was used for many games with counters as well as cards. The lyre-end sofa table in the corner of the room would be needed for writing IOUs for those who had lost heavily at cards.

DAIRY

I was first inspired to create a miniature dairy (see photograph opposite) after admiring well-presented examples of 18th- and 19th-century dairies at English stately homes that are open to the public. Uppark and Lanhydrock each have evocative examples of a way of life long gone. I was entranced by the cool, functional interiors of the dairies and the range of pottery utensils neatly laid out. This room setting would look out of place in a small house, but it could certainly add an extra dimension to a farmhouse or a country mansion.

MACKINTOSH ROOM

The work of Charles Rennie Mackintosh (1868–1928) has become more widely known and appreciated recently. In his own lifetime his designs astonished rather than impressed and were more valued by the avant garde in Europe than in his native Scotland.

A few years ago, I was able to see some of Charles Rennie Mackintosh's creations for myself on a visit to Glasgow, and became an instant admirer of his work. His hallmark of a strong, dark colour set against white can create a dramatic impression in miniature as well as in a full-size room. If your dolls' house is of an appropriate period, this is a style well worth trying out in one room. I created a small room to show off a few treasured miniatures in Mackintosh style, and the effect was as startling and attractive as I had hoped.

▲ This room is a homage to Mackintosh style. The background colour is part of a set of cards from an exhibition of his work. The wall plaque is a copy of one by Margaret Mackintosh, who worked with her husband to create stylish rooms that were years ahead of their time.

◀ Blue and white 'tiled' wallpaper and decorative wall panels provide the appropriate background for this dairy. The wooden butter churn is a working model: the handle can be turned.

LOFT CONVERSIONS

A loft or attic conversion is an excellent way to create extra living space in an existing house. Some dolls' houses are also suitable for this treatment, and if you have sufficient space under the roof, you have the potential for a delightful and unusual setting, given the odd shape of the room with its sloping walls. There are several options for the attic conversion, depending on the structure of your dolls' house, and the examples below may offer some practical ideas.

The lift-off roof on the house shown below reveals a floor space 26 x 8½in (660 x 215mm). The only thing needed to convert it into a perfect working space for an artist or designer was to fit a planked floor (see page 96). With the slope of the walls when the roof is in position, only the central portion of the floor can be used for furnishings, so careful positioning of any tall furniture is necessary.

Some dolls' houses have hinged roofs, and in the simpler ones the loft may not even have a floor. One can easily be added, and the resulting floor space divided into two rooms with a triangular piece of wood, adding further flexibility to the new space. Adding a non-opening door at the back will convey the impression of a staircase, or of other rooms behind (see the photograph on page 87).

If you are unable to resist adding some 1/24-scale furniture and accessories to a collection of mainly 1/12-scale miniatures, a loft space is the perfect place in which to arrange them, separated from the main house where they would be inappropriate.

◀ Lift-off roof and attic space.

◀ The removable roof panel in my Wealden house. The furniture in this loft space is all in 1/24 scale.

Another option is a removable roof panel that lifts off to reveal a small loft space, as in the photograph. You can leave the resulting room looking quite rough and ready, or smarten it up to the standard of the rooms below. For this house, I fitted a planked floor and finished the square opening for the stair-ladder with thin stripwood. I also added stripwood, varnished to match the exterior half-timbering on the house, to make a feature of the interior gable ends. The roof beams are ⅜in (10mm) square dowelling.

◀ The furnished attic room.

4

Shops

A shop can be an entertaining alternative to a miniature home, as it can be adapted easily to a specific interest. Dolls' house shops are no more expensive than houses, and prices vary according to the size and detailing. An antique shop, for example, can include furnishings and household goods of many different periods; a specialist shop could be ideal for the collector of miniature ceramics or woodturned objects which can be displayed on shelves and tables.

A shop is the perfect way to show off your own handiwork if you enjoy a particular craft, be it miniature needlepoint carpets and cushions, pictures, or samplers. Your shop can stock anything you choose, depending on the space available; you could even use a room box. This section includes ideas for shops using a wide range of miniatures. For practical tips on fitting out your shop see page 48.

◄ The single-room corner basket shop is designed to evoke a feeling of French country life. The baskets, in a variety of traditional styles, were woven by an English maker who lives in France. The shop base extends far enough to allow some of the stock to be displayed outside. A table and shelves for the use of the shop owner can be glimpsed through one of the windows.

ANTIQUE SHOP

An antique shop can hold a vast range of objects: again your only limit is the space available. If you occasionally buy furniture or ornaments on impulse to keep for some future project, they can be kept in the shop for safe storage as well as for display, although you may never get round to moving them to their intended home. The shop can be full of expensive-looking fine furniture, or it could be more like a junk shop, according to your taste and the budget you have fixed.

You will probably want to include some display shelves, and these are simple to make (see page 120). A top hat, a parasol and perhaps a pretty shawl might be displayed over an antique chair. Books can be neatly arranged on shelves or left in piles on the floor to add a suitably musty feel. You can make a whole collection of non-opening books inexpensively from a packet of coloured printed covers, available from dolls' house shops and suppliers. These simply need cutting out carefully and glueing round a small block of balsawood.

▲ An old-fashioned perambulator can form part of the stock in an antique shop and is also useful for displaying dolls or, as in this case, teddy bears.

◄ Shelves fitted across the entire back wall of the shop provide storage for an assortment of decorative 'antiques'.

FLORIST

A florist's shop offers splendid opportunities for display. Miniature flowers seem almost prettier than the real thing when arranged in vases or pots, or less formally as bunches filling buckets. Lids from perfume sprays, hand lotions and lipsticks can also be used as containers.

Flowers that have been hand-made by professional miniaturists are exquisite: we may marvel at the makers' skill in producing such realism. Kits are also available for you to make your own flowers, and if you are neat-fingered and patient, you can choose from many different blooms. Good eyesight – or the use of a magnifying glass – is essential. Pots of daffodils can be arranged outside a shop to add colour.

▼ This attractive flower shop is arranged in an original idea for a kit that provides both a dwelling house and a shop with living accommodation above.

ART GALLERY

If one of your hobbies is for collecting or even painting miniature works of art, why not create a gallery? There will be far more space to display your treasures than in a dolls' house full of furniture. Pictures look best hung in groups, and very superior ones can be displayed individually on easels. Ready-made miniature frames are easy to obtain, or you can take on the task of framing the pictures yourself (see page 133).

▲ The exterior of the gallery. A beautifully-painted façade and some architectural additions transform a plain shop into a work of art in itself.

◀ Inside the shop. The stock is laid out to appeal to the customer who might patronize such a fashion-conscious establishment. Colour schemes have been chosen to give a coordinated effect when the shop is open to view.

INTERIOR DESIGN SHOP

This dolls' house is based on an 18th-century shop. I decorated the façade in typical Georgian style and colours, but inside it is a modern interior design and decoration store. This allowed me to fill it with an assortment of frivolous and pretty objects, both bought and home-made. Its contents, inspired by ideas in interior design magazines and trendy shops in London and Bath, will eventually be a tiny time capsule of decorative themes. Depending on what takes your fancy, you could stock this kind of shop with bales of material, cushions, rugs, rolls of wallpaper, ornaments or small items of furniture.

▲ My two-storey Georgian shop offers opportunities to arrange imaginative displays, and accommodation 'over the shop' if required.

SPECIAL SHOP DETAILS

If you are fitting out a shop rather than a house, there are several specific items you will need to arrange, apart from basic decoration and contents. A traditional shop should have a bell to alert the shopkeeper to customers. Attach a small one just above the door, suspended from a hook by a thin wire, so that it tinkles when the door is opened and closed. Don't forget to make an 'open' and 'closed' sign to hang on the door.

▶ A hanging sign is a good way to attract custom. Attach a metal bracket to the wall with superglue. The sign can be handwritten, or it could be a picture.

THE SHOP NAME

You can make a suitable name for your shop in several ways. One is to use a lettering stencil, which will give you a choice of type style. The lettering can be outlined on a piece of card and coloured in using a gold pen or a black marker pen. Take care when you are spacing stencilled letters, and look at some real examples first. Make base and top lines with masking tape so that your letters are in a straight line. Another way to produce impressive lettering is by using the self-adhesive gold letters made to personalize luggage. Attach them with adhesive putty first, then adjust the spacing if necessary before fixing them in place permanently.

◀ Not everyone is a talented signwriter, and making a suitable shop fascia board sometimes causes problems. I have used stencilling and self-adhesive letters, but in this case my daughter and son-in-law, both graphic artists, gave me the shop name as a Christmas present.

If you have a computer and a printer, the simplest option is to choose a suitable typeface and then set it in a large font size. Make trial prints until you have a version that looks good when trimmed and held in place on the shop front. Print the final version on thin, shiny card, or on shiny paper which can be pasted on card, trimmed to size and glued in place.

WINDOW DISPLAYS

A good window display is vital for any shop: it is the first thing to catch the eye. Window dressing is a special skill. Next time you go shopping, study the displays and see what makes an interesting window rather than a dull one. You can give height to your arrangement by fitting shelves; adapt the method for simple bookshelves on page 120 as necessary. Small acrylic boxes make excellent display stands. Add a length of thin brass tube on which you can hang suitable miniatures.

Displays of food
If you decide to have a food shop, a wide choice of food miniatures is available, or you can make your own – see page 36 for more details.

To make earthy potatoes for a greengrocer's display, model small, potato-shaped balls from modelling compound and harden in the oven in the usual way. Brush with glue and roll the potatoes in railway modeller's earth flock powder. Shake off the excess to give a natural look.

◄ The window display of this curio shop is arranged to show off ornaments and sparkling glass, and looks equally enticing from both inside and outside. The striped wallpaper and the rope-twist border round the window helps to establish the look of a seaside souvenir shop.

5

Houses for children

Providing a house for a child can be a delightful introduction to the world of the dolls' house. There are few constraints on period: imagine and create anything that will please the new home owner. There are important points to consider, however, as the child will treat the house as a plaything, rather than a showcase. A decorative theme for a child's dolls' house may stem from a favourite toy, a story, or something that he or she likes to collect.

THREE TO FIVE YEARS

Dolls' houses stocked by toy shops rather than specialist dolls' house shops, or sold by mail order by many toy manufacturers, are specifically designed for young children. It is vital that a dolls' house intended for play should be sturdy and not easily damaged. If the child is under five, try to find a house that is open-plan and accessible from both back and front, so that it can be played with by two or three children together. This type of house is usually sold flat-packed, and tends to be relatively inexpensive. The usual scale is 1/12, though houses for very young children may be in 1/10 scale.

▶ The vivid colour of ready-decorated Camellia Cottage is guaranteed to appeal to this age group. The flat-pack kit is also decorated on the inside and can be assembled very quickly, ensuring that it will be ready for a birthday or Christmas present even if you are short of time. It has three floors including an attic, and a central staircase so that the doll inhabitants can more realistically go upstairs. At 24in wide x 12in deep x 26in high (610 x 305 x 660mm) it allows two children to play together amicably.

FIVE TO EIGHT YEARS

For children aged five years and upwards, a house with a prettily-decorated front will be popular. Fixtures and fittings need to be sturdy, but some more delicate items can be added as the children become more dextrous and interested in detail.

▷ Primrose Cottage, with its attractive windows and door, will suit this age-group, who like a little more realism than when they were younger. The kit is designed for ease of assembly, and glue, screws and hinges are all supplied. All you need to provide is a screwdriver.

NINE YEARS AND ABOVE

For children aged nine years or more, it is worth investing in a proper, 1/12-scale house. If the child becomes interested in the dolls' house as a hobby, inexpensive first furniture can be replaced gradually with more 'collectable' items.

◁ A traditional three-storey house with generously-sized rooms, Vine House can be extended with the addition of a basement complete with steps and railings when the young owner needs more space to fill.

DECORATION AND FITTINGS

Even if the house is intended as a Christmas or birthday surprise, it is probably best not to decorate it completely. Why not let the child become involved right from the start? He or she will enjoy the house far more if allowed to contribute, and a large part of the pleasure of owning a dolls' house is to fit out the inside. It is not beyond the capabilities of an average eight-year-old to help to make curtains, fit carpets or even paper walls, with a little help and guidance.

It is best not to use expensive mouldings to start with, as a child will not appreciate beautifully mitred joints. Instead, use plain stripwood from a model shop, which is much cheaper, and butt it together at the corners to provide simple skirting boards. Use general purpose adhesive rather than permanent wood glue, so that these mouldings can be removed later and replaced with better-quality materials, when the child is ready to enjoy the detail.

IDEAS FOR DECORATION

No decorative feature in a child's dolls' house need be expensive. A satisfactory effect can be achieved very easily with the most mundane of materials.

- Make stair carpet using furnishing braid fixed with double-sided tape, which is easily replaced during redecoration.

- Make an open staircase 'safe' with a side panel of needlepoint canvas. Brush with all-purpose glue to make it stiffer, and paint it white.

- Make an elaborate plasterwork ceiling from a small paper doily. Base-coat the ceiling with emulsion, allow to dry, then glue on the doily carefully. Apply a second coat of emulsion, working gently so that the doily does not tear.

- Adorn walls and mantelpieces with tiny pictures cut from magazines, glued to jewellery 'frames'.

- Use old clip earrings to hold back curtains or bed canopies.

TUDOR HOUSE

The popular mock-Tudor, half-timbered style will be familiar to many children (some of whom live in such homes as many were built, especially in England). The beamed and gabled façades have all the attractions of the original Tudor style from which they derive, but can be furnished in a style similar to a modern-day home.

Half-timbered houses always seem to appeal to children, as they do to many adults. It is possible to obtain inexpensive and hard-wearing models with the beams screen-printed on the façade. Inside you can decorate by hanging paper 'tapestries' cut from magazines on the wall. The lid of a small jar can be used to hold pot pourri (regular pot pourri shredded into smaller pieces). An inexpensive plastic chandelier will look impressive.

▲ Oak Hurst is a delightful reproduction of mock-Tudor style, complete with entrance porch and leaded windows, and although I recommend this house for a child, it will also appeal to many adults.

CASTLE

Interest in dolls' houses is certainly not confined to small girls. Boys are often fascinated by anything miniature, especially if this includes items with moving parts. They may enjoy playing with a dolls' house just as much as the girls. A house for a boy can be based on any theme of special interest or a current hobby, whether it is a sport or collecting.

A castle will appeal to both boys and girls. It makes a good setting for battle scenes, while the turret room is suitable for any princess who needs to be rescued.

◀ This splendid Gothic-inspired castle can be built from a basic kit; a lighting set and decoration pack are available as an option. It can become the inspiration for hours of imaginative play.

FURNITURE

Some commercially-made dolls' house furniture sold in toy shops and department stores is in 1/16 scale. This is a legacy of the old Tri-ang dolls' houses (see page 152) and a later make, Caroline's Home, which some readers may remember.

In general, young children are not worried by inconsistencies of scale, though older children may find it important as they often like to have everything just so. A mixture of ready-made furniture, home-made items and some plain, strong wooden furniture that can be painted or stencilled by the child, are ideal for a first dolls' house. Nothing needs to be expensive, so that it will not be a tragedy when breakages occur.

▲ A cradle made from a walnut shell, or a small wooden box as shown, will give great pleasure, especially if it contains a tiny baby doll. The doll can be a small bead, marked to resemble a face, attached to a basic cloth body and wrapped in scraps of lace. The bowls are acorn cups painted gold, while the tiny rabbits may be preferred to dolls by a small child who is fond of animals.

▲ Christmas festivities and decorations can be enjoyed to the full in the miniature scale.

DOLLS' HOUSE CHRISTMAS

Children invariably become excited around Christmas time, and most love to be involved in preparations, decorating and general hustle and bustle. Why not extend it to the dolls' house? If children have a house of their own, they can have enormous fun decking it out with miniature decorations, which they can make themselves, with a bit of help. If you own an 'adult' collectors' dolls' house, and have time to spare, you could decorate that too, perhaps at the last minute as a surprise for the children on Christmas Day.

MINIATURE CHRISTMAS DECORATIONS

- Fix a wreath to the front door.

- Make a miniature Christmas tree: a section from a bottle brush, dyed green and sprinkled with glitter, works well.

- Make special miniature festive food using modelling compound.

- Cut out small stocking shapes from one thickness of felt and hang near the fireplace.

- Crochet a 'paper-chain' from gilt parcel string, or two strands of embroidery cotton in either red or green.

- Make Christmas cards by cutting out small details from used cards. Some Christmas catalogues have mini-reproductions of cards.

- Make a pile of parcels using small blocks of wood or boxes in different sizes, wrapped in coloured shiny paper.

▲ These Christmas decorations and food are all professionally made. Just like our full-sized decorations, they are carefully packed away each year, ready for when Christmas comes round again.

THE INHABITANTS

'People' are essential for a child's house. They need not be dolls: very young children might prefer small, furry animals, miniature mice, or teddy bears. An older child will probably want a family of dolls. Peg dolls are inexpensive and easy to make from old fashioned, wooden clothes pegs, but the disadvantage of the standard peg doll is that it cannot sit down.

Watching my grandchildren playing with their dolls' houses, I realised how important such things are. If they want to arrange a tea party, or sit the doll on a chair, a stiff, stand-up doll simply will not do. It is not difficult to make sit-down peg dolls, which can be dressed in any way you wish. Instructions are given on page 115.

PRACTICAL MATTERS

6

Equipment and materials

You will need a certain amount of equipment for working on your dolls' house. You may already have some of the items mentioned in this section, but it is likely that you will have to buy others. My advice is to buy the best quality you can afford.

In my experience, once you have tasted the satisfaction of completing your first dolls' house, you are likely to want to go on to the next and will need your tools again and again. This list should help you to choose wisely.

ESSENTIAL TOOLS

For the initial preparation and exterior decoration of your house you will need the following:

- Glasspaper, grades 00 to 3

- Interior plaster filler

- Orange stick

- Emery board

- Good quality paintbrushes, sizes ½in (13mm), ¾in (19mm) and 1in (25mm)

- Fine art paintbrushes for small details, sizes 00 to 3 and size 5

Sanding
Wrap glasspaper round a small block of wood to avoid rounding off corners. Do not go on using glasspaper which is worn, as it will be ineffective. An emery board (the kind used for nail care) is perfect for smoothing the corners of window frames, door frames and glazing bars. It will go into tight corners and can also be used while you are painting: if you see a slight bump missed in the earlier sanding, rub it down with the emery board and paint over it to produce a really smooth finish.

You will need these basic tools to fit out the interior of the house:

- Small screwdrivers (the size used for small electrical work)

- Bradawl (a pointed tool for starting a hole in wood to insert screws)

  Note: a thick darning needle is often sufficient to start a hole in soft wood. Protect your thumb with a thimble.

- Craft knife

  Note: a good pair of scissors is adequate for some purposes, but a craft knife is far more effective for cutting perfectly straight lines on paper or card.

- Metal ruler with a raised edge for use as a cutting guide

- Self-healing cutting mat marked with a squared grid (from stationers or suppliers of art materials)

  Note: using the grid on a cutting mat saves both time and trouble when cutting parallel edges.

- Metal mitre box and saw

  Note: A good combination is X-Acto mitre box no. 7533 and knife handle no. 5, fitted with saw blade no. 239. Other makes, all of a fairly standard size, are available from suppliers of miniature tools)

- Gent's saw, 7in (180mm) long

- Pencils

  Note: Sharpen pencils often, as even the width of the line made by a blunt pencil will make measurements inaccurate.

- Bulldog clips

- Masking tape

- Magnifier for checking fine detail

▲ Tools and glues can be stored away neatly inside the dolls' house while work is in progress. An egg-cup makes a useful container for tiny screws.

Working with sharp tools

Treat all cutting tools with respect. For safety, craft knife blades must be changed frequently; they are inexpensive and are only effective when sharp. Use a raised-edge metal ruler as a guide. If you cut acetate for window glazing, change the blade as soon as you have finished, as it will be blunt.

Rule 1
To avoid accidents, always check before you cut that your free hand is behind the blade and not in front of it.

Rule 2
Never use cutting tools if you are tired, when it becomes too easy to make a mistake. There is always another day.

Rule 3
Always put your craft knife down if you check or adjust the position of the work. It is easy to forget that you are holding it and nick yourself.

ADHESIVES

You will need to use a variety of adhesives, depending on the task in hand. Modern adhesives are not interchangeable and work best on the materials for which they were developed. Most produce fumes to some extent so it is essential to work in a well-ventilated room, preferably with the window open. This guide shows which are suitable for different materials.

Glue fumes

Glue fumes are definitely not good for you, whether you notice them or not, and exposure to concentrated amounts can be dangerous. I have been in one dolls' house maker's workshop where the fumes were so strong that I found it difficult to breathe. The craftsman did not even notice the effect, probably due to repeated exposure.

Type of glue	Where and how to use
ALL-PURPOSE CLEAR ADHESIVE	For card, paper, wood and ceramics
PVA WHITE WOOD ADHESIVE	For permanent fixing of wood; once set, the bond cannot be undone
LATEX-BASED ADHESIVE	To attach ceramic tiles to card or wood; do not use on fabrics as this type of glue yellows with age
EPOXY RESIN	An extra-strong, all purpose glue that is mixed from two tubes before use; it will provide an exceptionally strong bond on small parts, such as metal feet attached to wooden legs on furniture
POLYSTYRENE CEMENT	Useful for the dolls' house garden as it does not dissolve polystyrene (used to make fake rocks)
PAPER GLUE	Use on thick paper only as it is easy to over-wet paper and produce a crinkled effect. Useful for fixing flock powder in the dolls' house garden
SUPERGLUE	Use with care to attach ceiling roses, etc. Rinse off fingers before touching anything. Use tweezers when attaching small parts

PREPARATION

Although decorating a dolls' house is much less tiring than full-size decoration, it is certainly more fiddly and care is needed to achieve a perfect result. It is vital to prepare the surface well, because in such a small scale any tiny blemish or hairline crack will show up badly after decoration. The list of tools you will need is on page 58.

Sand all surfaces with fine glasspaper and fill any cracks with interior plaster filler. An orange stick is the best thing to use for pushing filler right into the joints. When this has set, sand smooth and remove any loose dust.

Next, undercoat the exterior and interior walls, even if you plan to wallpaper certain rooms. This will prevent any marks or colour in the wood from showing through later. It is worth rubbing over the undercoat, when dry, with size 00 glasspaper.

Topcoat the ceilings with emulsion paint.

▲ A miniature electric drill is not essential and is an expensive extra if you plan only one dolls' house, but for the committed hobbyist it makes fitting door knobs or hinges much easier.

Using filler

It is difficult to mix an amount of filler small enough for most dolls' house work. It is possible to keep filler workable for a short time by gathering what is left into a lump and wrapping it closely in damp clingfilm. If you prefer to use ready-mixed interior filler, be warned that this, too, dries up if exposed to air. Take out a small quantity from the carton and put it in an egg-cup while working, resealing the carton.

PAINT

The list is a guide to the best paints to use on different parts of your dolls' house.

Type of paint	Where to use
EMULSION PAINT	Interior walls, ceilings and as undercoat on thin wood mouldings. Emulsion is available in sample pots, which are often a suitable size for dolls' house decoration
GLOSS PAINT	Do not use on a dolls' house, with the possible exception of the front door. The excessive shine looks unrealistic in small scale
SEMI-MATT PAINT	Satin finish is best for exterior walls, door and window frames, roofs and interior paintwork
MODEL ENAMEL	Useful on its own or mixed with emulsion to make more interesting colours for roofs, ornaments and accessories. Available from craft shops
GOUACHE	A small amount mixed with emulsion and diluted with a splash of water will produce glowing colours for walls and roofs (see page 66) to simulate colour-washed cob or plaster. The mix will not be waterproof and must be finished with a coat of matt or semi-matt varnish. Available from suppliers of artists' materials
ACRYLIC	Can be mixed to make realistic shades for roof tiles or slates (see page 74). Available from hobby shops or suppliers of artists' materials

LIGHTING

The effect of a beautifully-lit dolls' house is magical. If you wish to install electric lighting in yours, the best plan is to fit it before decorating so that any wires can be concealed. Booklets which will take you through every stage of the installation are available by mail order and from dolls' house shops. Provided you follow the manufacturer's instructions, fitting the system is within the capabilities of a beginner. If you are prepared to undertake occasional maintenance work, installing lighting will definitely be worth the effort.

The easiest way to tackle lighting is to buy a kit designed to suit the number of rooms you have. Kits work from a 12-volt battery or a transformer. Copper tape wires can be fixed to the floors and concealed under any floor covering. Skirting boards are available with a groove cut in the back to take the wires.

If you do not have a transformer, there will be some future expense in replacing batteries from time to time. Changing tiny bulbs in a restricted space can be difficult unless you are dextrous. If a fault occurs in concealed wiring, you may have to redecorate after you have located and repaired it.

▲ Interior lighting in this 18th-century Gothic folly provides a touch of magic.

TWENTY STEPS TO BASIC DECORATION

You are bound to be impatient to start on the decoration of your new dolls' house, but it pays not to be in too much of a hurry. Care and thought at each stage will ensure good results. Before you begin decorating, it is important to prepare surfaces. Unless the house is to be no more than a series of boxes joined together, you will probably want to install some fixtures and fittings.

The check list opposite gives my 'twenty steps' to basic decoration and sets out a logical order for work. Detailed instructions for each process follow the initial list, together with step-by-step guides for making basic fixtures. The woodwork required for such additions is simple for the beginner, using the tools listed on page 59. If you are really averse to tackling woodwork of any kind, there are ways you can overcome this, perhaps by using braid instead of cornices or dado rails. A range of simple paint finishes is given on page 62, and for the more ambitious, a variety of more elaborate decorative treatments is shown on pages 72–77.

▼ A shop with living accommodation above provides plenty of scope for the hobbyist to arrange the interior in an individual way. This shell provided the basis for my interior design shop (see page 47).

◀ This is the interior of the shop. My original intention was to use the lower part as a shop and have a living room and bedroom above, but during the planning stage I changed my mind and decided to devote the entire building to display space.

TWENTY STEPS CHECK LIST

Preparation

1 Smooth over both exterior and interior surfaces using fine glasspaper

2 Fill any cracks with filler and leave to dry. Interior plaster filler is better for this purpose than wood filler as it is finer. Sand again

3 Make sure the house is free of dust before you begin painting. If possible use a suction cleaner with a fine nozzle attachment

4 Paint both exterior and interior walls with quick-drying primer or undercoat

5 Apply two coats of emulsion to the ceilings. One coat is sufficient at this stage if you plan to add any special treatment later

Exterior decoration

6 Paint the exterior walls and the roof (see page 66)

7 Paint the window frames and the door frames (see pages 69–70)

8 Paint the front door (door furniture such as a knob, letterbox or a knocker can be fitted at this stage, or when all the decoration has been completed)

Interior design (grey numbers are optional additions)

9 Fit lighting (see page 63)

10 Make / fit chimney breasts (see pages 82–83).

11 Make fireplaces (see page 79–83)

12 Make staircase additions such as balusters, newel posts or side panel (see pages 85–87)

13 Fit flooring (see pages 88–91)

14 Fit internal doors (see pages 95–96)

Interior decoration

15 Paint walls in chosen colours (see page 100)

16 Wallpaper walls (see pages 101–104)

17 Add wallpaper borders (see pages 105)

Fittings

18 Fit door frames (see page 92)

19 Cut, paint and fit skirtings, cornice and dado rail or picture rail (see pages 92–94)

20 Cut and fit window glazing and internal window frames if required (see page 69–70)

7

Exterior finishes

Model enamels can give an excellent finish on a plain roof. You will need the larger can for most roofs, as two coats are necessary to give a good overall covering. A matt-finish medium grey will suit most dolls' houses. Paint exterior walls with two coats of satin finish semi-matt paint in the colour of your choice. Any architectural features can be added at a later stage. For details of special paint finishes and textured treatments see opposite, and also pages 76–77.

COLOURED ROOFS

A strong colour can also be a good choice for a roof. The one on my Wealden house was copied from a painting of a Kentish house in sunlight, which made the reddish-brown tiles glow bright orange. This colour was also made with gouache, this time using orange and a little yellow ochre mixed with magnolia emulsion. The chimney was painted with the same basic mix as the walls but with some brown added to give a smoke-darkened effect. Use the technique described on page 68.

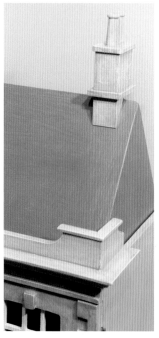

◄ This Cotswold house roof was painted using the same method as for the Wealden house (pictured below). A mix of buff emulsion and gouache in olive green and mid-grey was used over a buff emulsion basecoat, to complement the warm yellow 'stone' walls.

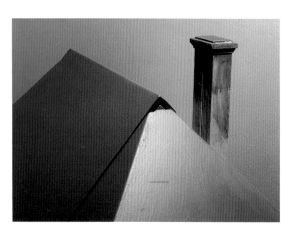

◄ The vibrant colour of the roof of the Wealden house was achieved using a gouache mix.

TEXTURED FINISHES

If you want to create an effect on the exterior walls of your house that goes beyond mere colour, there are a number of ways to add texture. Two are described here:

PEBBLEDASH

Pebbledash was a highly popular finish for suburban houses that were built in England during the 1930s and 1940s. To reproduce the effect, glue sheets of coarse sandpaper (grade 2) to the walls, rough side outwards, and paint over them with white or pale grey emulsion. Before painting, conceal joins using interior filler applied with an orange stick.

COB OR PLASTER

Originally a building material made of clay and chopped straw, cob can be replicated as an effect on a 1/12-scale cottage. Textured masonry paint, used to paint and weatherproof real house walls, is ideal for use on small-scale properties, but unless you already have some (perhaps left over from full-scale decorations) a large can will be unnecessarily expensive. It is possible to make up your own textured paint by mixing interior plaster filler with white emulsion paint, diluted with a very small amount of water. The magic extra ingredient is PVA white wood glue. Stir in a small amount and your mixture will bond with the house wall and never flake off. This finish is permanent and cannot be removed. Try a test piece on spare wood first if possible.

◀ Black-and-white half-timbered houses look spectacular, but in line with current thoughts on conservation, a more subtle effect is achieved with pink or ochre walls and natural oak beams. I used chestnut stain for the beams on this house, which show up well but are not too dark.

EXTERIOR WALLS

Houses in cob or plaster are often colour-washed, and these effects are not difficult to reproduce in 1/12 scale. The best way to achieve a suitably warm, intense colour is to mix regular emulsion paint with a small amount of gouache. This method makes the warm ochre colour used for my Kentish Wealden house (see page 67). It is also suitable for a cottage or farmhouse, or you could use the same technique with different colours to suit your own dolls' house.

Materials

1 tube of yellow ochre gouache
1 tube sandstone gouache
Magnolia emulsion (enough for undercoat and top coat)
1in (25mm) paintbrush (preferably well-used, as it needs to be stiff – a square-ended stencil brush is also suitable)
Small piece of cotton rag
Matt varnish

Adjacent surfaces

If you need to paint and varnish on adjacent surfaces, for example on a half-timbered house, apply the varnish first. You can paint over varnish if there is a smudge in the wrong place, but you cannot varnish over a spot of paint.

Method

1 Apply a base coat of emulsion to the exterior walls. Paint a small piece of wood or firm card too, as a tester.

2 Mix a very small amount of both the yellow ochre and the sandstone gouache into half a pint (250ml) of the magnolia emulsion. Test the colour on the base-coated wood or card. Adjust if necessary, then thin the mixture with a little water.

3 Begin painting on the back of the house to judge the effect. The emulsion/gouache mixture is water soluble, and if you are not happy with the colour, it can be wiped off with a damp rag and the mix adjusted before starting again.

4 When you are happy with the colour, paint one wall at a time and immediately rub some of the fresh paint off with a dry rag. For a natural-looking finish, you want to achieve a slightly patchy effect, with some of the base coat showing through. It is important to work quickly, painting and rubbing each wall in turn, as the mix dries rapidly.

5 Finish with a coat of matt varnish to seal the colour and make it waterproof. This will darken the shade slightly: if you want to check the finished colour first, you will need to varnish the test card too, before painting the walls of the house. You will almost certainly find, however, that the slight darkening is not enough to worry about.

WINDOWS AND DOORS

Windows are often supplied with a dolls' house, already screen-printed with white glazing bars or black, diamond-shaped panes to suit the style of the house, and instructions for fitting will be provided.

When painting the glazing bars on fixed-in windows, it is easy to miss the underneath or one side of some of the bars. The best way to avoid this is to establish an order of work: paint the underneath and one side of each section in sequence, then the other side and lastly the top of each. This will prevent the irritation when coming back to admire your work later, only to find that some parts have been missed. If you have not done much painting, you might like to try out a practice piece on a spare bit of wood first, to test your skills in achieving a smooth finish.

▲ This house in the late Regency style has features resembling those described in Jane Austen's novels. The pillared portico adds an air of distinction, and this kit provides the choice of door and window frames in wood or white plastic that does not need painting.

GLAZING

If you have to make your own windows, use plain acetate (available from hobby shops). The sheets are about 8 x 10in (205 x 250mm) and are protected on both sides by a peel-off film to prevent them being scratched before use.

Be economical with the glue and wait until it is tacky before fixing the acetate in place. Keep an orange stick and some white spirit handy. If you accidentally smear some on the acetate you can wipe it off if you act immediately.

Method

1. Remove the protective film from the acetate sheet. Cut the acetate 6mm (¼in) larger all round than the window space so that it will overlap on each edge.

2. Apply a tiny amount of all-purpose glue to the wall around the window aperture. Leave for a few seconds to become tacky.

3. Press the glazing gently into place. Take care not to slide it about, or the glue will leave a trail on the clean surface.

Cutting acetate
Take extra care when cutting with a craft knife and metal raised-edge ruler, as acetate is very slippery. The knife blade can easily skate over the surface if not held firmly. Acetate of the correct weight is a little too thick to cut comfortably and neatly using scissors.

WINDOW FRAMES

Complete internal window frames are not necessary if you plan to add curtains and pelmets, but to make the window look finished it is usually best to glue on a thin strip of wood below it to form a window-sill. If you plan to fit blinds, add thin stripwood or moulding at the sides and a sill at the bottom. There is no need to mitre any corners: it is simplest to make the sill extend slightly beyond the side frames.

Clearance

Before adding window frames, check that there is sufficient clearance for them when the house is closed. If windows are sited near the front edge of one of the walls of a room, the addition of a frame or even a curtain, might prevent the house from closing properly. In this case, edge the window with a wallpaper border instead.

◄ This exquisitely detailed window was made for a house based on Robert Adam's own home in London, long since demolished. Adam's original drawings still exist.

SHOP WINDOWS

A shop window needs a complete frame inside as there will be no curtains. Mitre the corners of the wooden mouldings as described for fireplace mouldings (see page 79). Surround with a wallpaper border as an extra decorative and finishing feature.

FRONT DOOR

The front door is such an important feature of any house that it is worth taking trouble to make sure that it is of a suitable style and properly decorated.

The choice of colour for a front door is very personal. For a Tudor or Jacobean house the choice will be made for you: the door should be stained or varnished to resemble oak. Use of gloss paint should be restricted to a black front door for a Victorian town house, or a brightly coloured door for a child's dolls' house, otherwise semi-matt paint should be used.

White paint will accentuate any special details on a porch, and will make a feature of a pillared portico, especially if this is contrasted with a darker house wall.

▲ A planked oak door nestling under the overhanging, jettied storey of a timber-framed house is meticulously copied from an original building.

DOOR FURNITURE

If your house was supplied with a plain front door, it can be improved by the addition of attractive door furniture. A doorknob is usually fitted on a purchased dolls' house, and is supplied with a kit house. You could add a lion's-head knocker to the door of a country house, or an Adam-style brass doorknocker to a Georgian or Regency one. Houses of later periods may also have letter boxes, and carriage lamps may look good on either side of an imposing entrance. Doorknobs usually need to be screwed on, but doorknockers, letter boxes and bell pushes can be glued on with all-purpose glue. All these extras are available from dolls' house stockists.

▶ White against a dark green façade makes a striking contrast on a bow-windowed 18th-century shop front.

◀ A Georgian doorway with an attractive fanlight and classical columns on either side, faithfully copied from an 18th-century house in Bristol, England. The brickwork and even the railings on this house are made of wood.

SPECIAL FEATURES

Options for special paint finishes for house exteriors, both in terms of colour and texture, have already been covered (see pages 66–69). As well as painting, there are other ways to add interest to the exterior. Walls can be finished with sheets of cladding, all realistically coloured and textured, to provide instant wall-hung tiles, weatherboarding (siding) or brick. These sheets are available from dolls' house stockists and are simple to apply.

If you decide to use a plainer finish for the walls, you could consider a special finish for the roof. Sheets similar to the wall effects are available for a variety of roofing materials. Another option is tiny individual slates and tiles made of wood, fibre material or ceramic. They take time to apply, but are very realistic. The idea of gluing on several hundred minuscule tiles may seem daunting, but once you start it does not seem to take long and the result is highly satisfactory.

▲ Cut brick paper as shown left, including 'mortar' on one section only, so it can be butted against the next piece without showing a ridge. When you come to cut the second section (shown uncut, right) do this without the 'mortar' edging, to achieve an invisible join.

BRICK PAPER

Brick paper or plasticated sheet will give a good effect on many house styles. Care needs to be taken when making joins, which may be necessary when the size of the bricks does not fit exactly between the windows, or is not the full width of the house wall. One solution is to cover the outside edges with corner bricks or quoins (see page 76), but with other joins, it is important to make sure that the brick pattern fits exactly and that two half-bricks or two long bricks do not butt together.

◀ Shingles, weatherboard (siding) and wall tiles can be fixed quickly and in one piece.

SHINGLES

Wooden shingles come in a variety of shapes, so you can choose whichever style suits your house best. Apply stain before you glue the shingles on; they look best if the depth of colour is varied. Start with the bottom row: each row should overlap the one below by about ¼in (6mm). Stagger the shingles by starting each alternate row with a half-shingle. If necessary, they can be cut out with scissors to fit the rows exactly. Fix them on with wood glue.

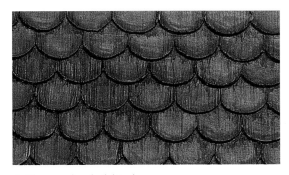

▲ Close-up detail of shingles.

SLATES

Individual miniature slates are usually made of fibre material in a suitable colour. They are lightweight and easy to fix in the same way as shingles.

◀ A selection of slates, tiles and other roof ornaments.

CERAMIC TILES

Ceramic roof tiles are a more expensive option, but are well worth it to finish off a special dolls' house. I decided to use Roman roof tiles on my 18th-century shop to match similar shops in Bath, which was first developed under Roman occupation, and where tiles like this are still used. This small roof needed about 350 tiles, so beware if you have a large house and limited time. I found the tiles simple to fix: they have shaped corners which means that the overlap slots cleanly into place. Ceramic tiles should be fixed with latex-based adhesive.

▲ These realistic Roman tiles make me think of sunny Italy, and are still a standard roofing material in Bath.

THE ECONOMY OPTION

For the effect of individual plain tiles or slates without the expense, you can make your own, using a railway modeller's method which works just as well on dolls' houses. Slates made of thin card are prepared in strips rather than individually, and are fixed with all-purpose glue. When in place, the slates can be painted with acrylic paint and varnished. After painting, you will be delighted with the transformation from humble card to realistic-looking slate.

Method

1 Cut strips of thin card about ¾ to 1in (20 to 25mm) deep, which can be joined to fit the length of the roof. An average strip length might be 8in (205mm) depending on the size of your roof.

2 Rule vertical pencil lines on the card strips at intervals of ⅝in (15mm) as in diagram 1.

3 Cut along each pencil line to within about ¼in (6mm) of the top of the strip. Cut small curves on the lower corners as in diagram 2. When the strips are overlapped on the roof, the visible part will resemble a row of slates.

4 Attach the strips to the roof using all-purpose adhesive, starting at the bottom and overlapping each row about ¼in (6mm) as for shingles. Stagger any joins between strips.

5 Finish the top of the roof with a plain strip of card approximately 1½ in(40mm) deep, folded in half lengthwise and glued along the ridge to cover the top row of slates as in diagram 3.

6 Use acrylic paint to transform the card into realistic-looking slates. A mixture of red, brown and yellow produces a warm russet colour; green, grey and yellow make pleasing slate-grey. Before you begin, make a shade card to keep handy, so that if you have not mixed enough paint it will be easy to match the colour of the next batch. Some slates here and there can be overpainted in a slightly darker shade to give some variation.

7 When the paint is dry, finish with a coat of matt varnish.

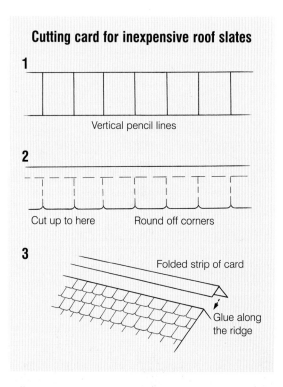

Cutting card for inexpensive roof slates

1
Vertical pencil lines

2
Cut up to here   Round off corners

3
Folded strip of card
Glue along the ridge

Card
Save card stiffeners from shirt or hosiery packaging to make slates. The card is just the right thickness.

THATCH

I am often asked how to imitate thatch, but there is no one solution: the answer is to experiment. There are as many ways of reproducing thatch as there are dolls' house makers and hobbyists who want to try it. Raffia or broom bristles can make a credible thatch: tie the material in bundles and glue these to the roof. Bundles can also be fixed with a staple gun. It is a time-consuming process and hard on the hands, though the finished result can be stunning. It helps to work with a picture of real thatch in front of you as an example.

As with slates, start with the bottom row and work upwards, so that each row overlaps the row below. Dormer windows are tricky to work round, so cover the section over each dormer separately before you tackle the main roof so that you can make an overlap at the top. Trim the edges neatly to shape with a pair of strong scissors, remembering that thatch always has rounded corners and should overhang the edge of the roof.

▼ This delightful limited-edition thatched cottage, complete with water wheel, is made from the most unlikely material: polyresin. It has a hard-wearing, moulded thatched roof and herringbone brick-effect walls. Inside are beamed ceilings and a gently curving staircase. The cottage is supplied complete and ready to furnish, but as it has so much fine detail, it is more expensive than an undecorated property. For hobbyists who do not want to decorate, it may be a dream come true.

CHIMNEYS

A good chimney makes all the difference to the appearance of a dolls' house roof. Chimneys can be tall and rectangular, short and square, with or without pots. If the chimney on your house seems too plain, the easiest thing to do is add some pots. Contrary to popular belief, chimneypots were installed on many Georgian houses, though it was during the Victorian period that whole rows of chimneypots became commonplace.

▲ A realistic chimney can be the finishing touch that makes a house look special. This authentic-looking brick-built chimney on a thatched cottage is finished with 'lead' flashing over the edge of the thatch.

ARCHITECTURAL FEATURES

If the outside of your house seems too plain, it can be transformed by adding accurate architectural details to the basic wall and roof decoration. Research suitable embellishments to avoid anachronisms before laying your plans.

QUOINS

Quoins are bricks used to emphasize the corners of a rectangular house. They make a smart contrast with brick walls or a plain painted finish. Ready-cut packs of 'quoining bricks' made from wood are available from dolls' house suppliers, but the quoins on the little house in the illustration are made of card. They are easy to make using these guidelines.

▲ A clear, bright colour picked out with white can make a simple house look special. Here, quoins have been added for emphasis. A weathervane on the roof completes the effect.

Proportions of small and full-size bricks for quoins.

Method

1   Measure the height of the house wall and divide the measurement into equal parts to decide the height of each brick. The exact size will depend on the height of the house, but an average is 1in (25mm) square for the larger brick and 1 x ½in (25 x 12mm) for the smaller, alternate bricks (see diagram left).

2   Cut the quoins individually from sturdy card and paint (white, off-white or stone colour) before attaching to the roof.

KEYSTONES

Shaped bricks can make an elegant, decorative flourish above the windows of a Georgian, Victorian or Edwardian house (see photograph on page 13). Like quoins, they can be made very simply in card.

Method

1 Exact measurements depend on the size of the house. Cut card shapes for each brick similar to those in the diagrams – three keystones for a small house, five for a grander effect.

2 Paint the cards before fixing. Keystones can be white as a contrast on a coloured wall, or brick colour on a brick house. Use matt-finish model enamel to reproduce brick.

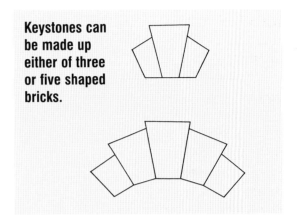

Keystones can be made up either of three or five shaped bricks.

PORCHES

Adding a porch is a simple way to transform the appearance of your house. Here are two attractive examples; see also pages 16 and 17.

▶ The small porch and keystone detail above this six-panelled door are typical of many houses in the English Cotswolds. The door is stained as oak.

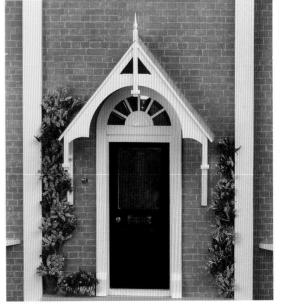

▲ A prettily-detailed porch and climbing plants provide a welcoming entrance.

8

Interior features

Without internal features, a dolls' house can seem a bit like a collection of boxes joined together. The difference is in the detail; features such as chimney breasts or fireplaces and staircases can give definition to a room and make your house appear far more realistic. You might also like to think about special flooring or details such as dado rails or cornices. Here are some ideas and practical advice that should inspire you to make your dolls' house a truly individual and personal creation.

CHIMNEY BREASTS AND FIREPLACES

Fitting a chimney breast is not obligatory. Fitting a fireplace directly on to the wall as though there is an exterior flue (see photograph, page 80) will work perfectly well. It is often the best option in a small bedroom where the bed will take up much of the space. Most sitting rooms, whatever the period of the house, look more interesting if the fireplace is fitted to a chimney breast. A chimney breast also provides useful alcoves on either side for display shelves, small items of furniture, or pictures. If you do want a chimney breast in a small room, fitting it in one corner saves space. These instructions will help you to make both standard and corner chimney breasts.

Before you make the chimney breast you should decide on the style and size of the fireplace. Beautifully-crafted fireplaces in various styles are available from dolls' house stockists. Some period rooms will look perfect with one of these elaborately

▲ An elegant fireplace with a marble surround and 'cast-iron' grate. The simple hearth (made from card covered with marbled paper) complements this style well.

'carved' fireplaces made in cast resin or plaster. If you do not wish to buy ready-made, you can design and build your own fireplace from pieces of wood mouldings, and you can make it as plain or elaborate as you wish.

BASIC FIREPLACE

Method

1 Decide on the size of your finished fireplace and plan it out on card.

2 Mitred joints are essential for a neat fit at the corners, so cut the moulding to length by placing in a mitre block with the plain back surface horizontal and cutting from the outer to the inner edge of the join (see diagram). Make sure that the two side pieces are exactly the same length.

3 Assemble the pieces using all-purpose adhesive.

4 Undercoat and topcoat with your chosen paint.

5 Cut the grate aperture on your card plan. Glue the tiles or marbled paper to the card to form the surround, and finally attach the actual fireplace.

Materials

Three lengths of wood moulding
Semi-matt finish paint of your choice
Marbled paper or tiles for grate surround
Stiff card

Cutting the mitred corners for a fireplace

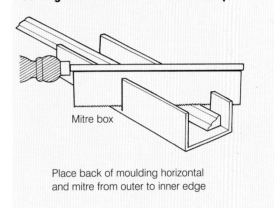

Mitre box

Place back of moulding horizontal
and mitre from outer to inner edge

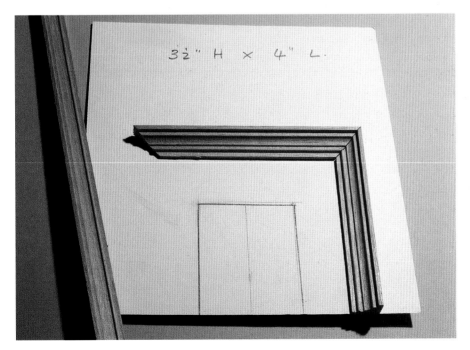

32" H × 4" L.

◀ I chose a deep cornice moulding for this simple fireplace. The height of the finished fireplace should relate to the height of the room. Make a cardboard cut-out and try it out in the room before you decide what will look best.

SIMPLE FIREPLACES

If, like me, you enjoy experimenting and want to produce a fireplace with a grander look, there are any number of possible variations. These can be made without cutting mitres.

REGENCY FIREPLACE

The fireplace is an important feature in a Regency room: this one is in the music room (see page 34). I used plain stripwood as a base and fancy mouldings for the top layer. Reeded wood and square panels with a circular central motif were both featured on Regency fireplaces.

The size of the fireplace can be varied to suit the room. The one shown is 4in (100mm) high and 4½in (115mm) long, plus the mantelshelf. Before you fit it to the wall, cut a piece of matt black card slightly larger than the aperture and glue to the back. Glue a strip of black card to the floor at the base of the aperture.

▲ The completed fireplace is fitted with a miniature Adam-style grate and a marbled card.hearth. Mouldings were made from a cut down 1/12 door frame, and the vase is a hand-painted copy of a Regency design.

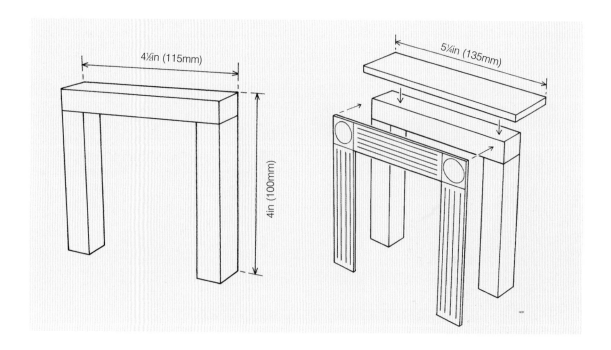

VICTORIAN FIREPLACE

Once you have made the basic fireplace, you will see how easy it is to make more complicated designs. This plain 'granite' fireplace is economical to make from oddments of left-over wood. You will need several thicknesses of wood strip. This example is 3¼in (80mm) wide and 3⅝in (90mm) high, but measurements can be altered to suit your room.

Method

1 Cut three pieces of ⅜in (10mm) dowelling, one 3½in (90mm) long for the top and two 3¼in (82mm) long for the sides. Glue them together.

2 Cut two pieces of ⅜in (10mm) right-angled stripwood each 3⅞in (98mm) long, and glue to the outsides of the side pieces of the basic shape.

3 Mark the centre and glue the mantelshelf on top, checking that it extends equally on either side.

4 To simulate granite, paint the fireplace with mid-grey matt model enamel. Streak and smudge with a darker grey. Only a few markings are needed.

◀ The finished fireplace.

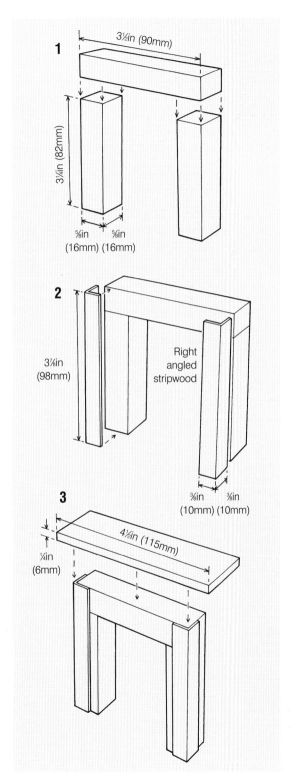

1 3½in (90mm)

3¼in (82mm)

⅝in (16mm) ⅝in (16mm)

2 3⅞in (98mm)

Right angled stripwood

⅜in (10mm) ⅜in (10mm)

3 4½in (115mm)

¼in (6mm)

BASIC CHIMNEY BREAST

Method

1 Measure the height of the room. The chimney breast should be the same height, and 1in (25mm) wider than the widest part of the planned fireplace (usually the mantelshelf), to allow about ½in (12mm) on either side.

2 Cut the balsawood or polyboard to size.

3 Using the fireplace as a guide, mark and cut an opening for the grate in the chimney breast, making sure that it is central (see diagram 1).

4 The sides and top of the grate opening should be black. Cut three small strips of matt black card about 1½in (40mm) wide, one measuring the same as the width of the opening and two measuring the same as its height. Fold and glue over the sides and top of the grate opening (see diagram 2). The card edges will be concealed at the back, and covered by the fireplace at the front.

5 Cut another piece of matt black card about 1in (25mm) deeper and wider than the opening. Glue this across the back of the chimney breast to cover the opening, leaving an overlap of ½in (12mm) all round, to make a fireback. Fold the spare ½in (12mm) of card at the base forwards, to make a floor for the grate (see diagram 3).

6 Check that the grate opening on the chimney breast and fireplace are the same size. Glue the chimney breast in place, and decorate along the rest of the room. Glue on the fireplace last.

Materials

Thin, matt black card
Balsawood, ½–¾in (13–20mm) thick (available from hobby shops)
or
Polyboard, a layer of foam sandwiched between two layers of card (available from art materials shops)

Note: balsawood and polyboard can be cut with a small saw or craft knife. Cut carefully as both crumble easily

Putting together a basic chimney breast.

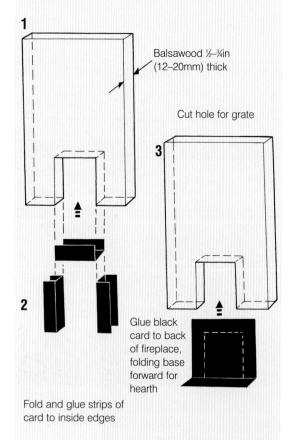

1
Balsawood ½–¾in (12–20mm) thick

Cut hole for grate

3

2
Fold and glue strips of card to inside edges

Glue black card to back of fireplace, folding base forward for hearth

CORNER FIREPLACE AND CHIMNEY BREAST

A space-saving corner chimney breast for a small room can be made from a piece of good-quality cardboard. The card fits diagonally across the corner of the room, leaving a gap behind.

Materials

Firm cardboard

Balsawood or polyboard

Matt black card

Prepared fireplace (small)

Beading/stripwood (optional)

▲ Planning a corner fireplace is a little more complicated: it should not be more than 3½in (90mm) wide, or it will take up too much floor space. The ends of the mantelshelf can fit neatly against the walls on either side. I used a thick piece of wood moulding for a base as a hearth would take up too much space.

▲ This striking Dutch-style fireplace has a surround fitted with replica Delft tiles. The plaster roundel above the fireplace and an elaborate tulip vase complete the effect.

Method

1 Measure the height of the room and the width of the angled space to be covered (fireplace width, plus ½in (12mm) either side). Cut the card the same height as the room and 3in (75mm) wider than the angled space.

2 Score the card 1½in (40mm) from each side edge and fold the two 'wings' back and inwards. These will be glued against the walls on either side (see diagram 1, over the page).

3 Cut a piece of balsawood or polyboard the same height as the chimney breast but 2in (50mm) narrower than the card. Glue this centrally to the back of the card to strengthen it (see diagram 1).

instructions continued overleaf

4 Cut an opening for the grate through both the card and the balsawood or polyboard. Finish with black card as for steps 4 and 5 of the basic chimney breast on page 80 (see diagram 2).

5 Fix the chimney breast in place by gluing the side wings to the walls on either side; the join can be covered by a thin strip of beading. Add the fireplace when decoration is complete.

Creating a corner chimney breast.

1 Back view

Corner of room

Flaps folded back, to be glued to the side walls

Space

Side wall

2 Grate

Extra balsawood or polyboard glued on for strength

Side wall

▶ A glowing fire is simple and quick to make. Fit a purchased grate or one made from a kit, or make a base for the fire from a piece of wood which can then be placed directly in the hearth.

MAKING A FIRE

An empty grate can look rather blank and unfriendly. It is easy to make a cheerful-looking fire, using the method given below, to create a homely atmosphere. Alternatively, why not put a miniature dried flower arrangement in the grate for a fresh, summery look?

Materials

Small piece of wood approximately ⅜in (10mm) thick
Railway modeller's coal or a few small twigs
Tube of red glitter
Scraps of red cellophane and gold paper

Method

1 Cut the wood to fit at the base of the fireplace, or inside a purchased grate. Paint the wood matt black, or use a black marker pen to colour it.

2 Cover alternately with all-purpose glue and coal, building up a good shape with several layers. Use twigs instead for a log fire.

3 Dab the arrangement with a little more glue and sprinkle generously with red glitter.

4 Add 'flames' at the back by gluing on small twists of the red cellophane and gold paper. One of each will probably be enough.

5 Allow the glue to set firm, then tap the fire to dislodge any loose glitter before placing it in the grate or on the hearthstone.

STAIRCASES

BALUSTERS

Some houses will be fitted with a staircase complete with balusters and handrail but you can add these to a basic flight of steps without too much trouble. Lengths of handrail, newel posts and packets of balusters are inexpensive and can be purchased from dolls' house suppliers. The handrail will have a groove cut on the underside to take balusters. These are often turned, but if you want a simpler and plainer look, perhaps for an early Georgian house, use ⅛in (3mm) square dowelling as 'stick' balusters.

Method

1 Before fitting, paint and varnish the balusters, newel posts and handrail in your desired style. Make sure everything has dried properly before moving on to the next stage.

2 Fit the top and bottom newel posts first, using all-purpose adhesive. Check with a set square that they are vertical. Leave overnight for glue to set.

3 Cut the handrail to size, cutting the ends at an angle to fit between the newel posts, and then glue in place.

4 To fit the balusters, cut the top of each at an angle to slot into the groove in the handrail. You may need to whittle away a little at the top for a neat fit. Glue in place.

Note: this may sound complicated, but once you start you will find that it is straightforward, if a little fiddly.

▲ The newel posts, balusters and handrail for this staircase are generally available in dolls' house shops. The effect was enhanced by a dado rail with white paint below and a cool green above. A wallpaper border accentuates the scheme.

Materials

1/12-scale handrails, newel posts and balusters in style and quantity required (allow 1 baluster for each step). Paint or varnish (white-painted balusters with mahogany handrail or pine-stained posts and handrail look stylish).

SIDE PANEL

For a modern house, or one which has been updated and is not strictly in period, you may wish to put in a side panel instead of balusters for the stairs.

Method

1 Cut newel posts from the square dowelling and glue in as on the previous method. An average post would be 3–4in (75–100mm) high, but this will depend on the ceiling heights in your house.

2 Cut a card pattern for the side panel and check the size before cutting the wood. The panel should be about 2½in (65mm) tall and long enough to fit neatly between the newel posts. The ends should be cut at an angle to enable the panel to fit properly up the slope of the stairs (see diagram 1). The average dolls' house staircase is steeper than a real one, so the angle is likely to be 45°.

3 Check that the wooden panel will fit correctly and paint or varnish it to match the surrounding decorations. Leave to dry and then glue in place (see diagram 2). If the hall and staircase are to be wallpapered, you can paper over the panel too, but this should be done after fitting, along with the rest of the decoration.

4 To make a neat edge at the base of the panel, glue a strip of thin wooden beading along the bottom, between the newel posts.

Materials

¼in (6mm) square dowelling
Firm card
Thin wood such as jelutong, or rigid cardboard
Paint or varnish
Wooden beading (optional)

Fitting a side panel for a staircase

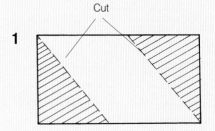

Cut

1

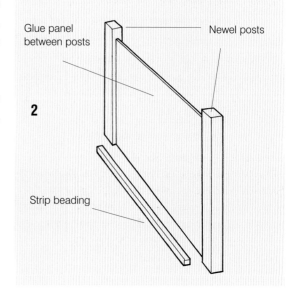

Glue panel between posts

Newel posts

2

Strip beading

SIMPLE HANDRAIL

Some dolls' house staircases are boxed in between the outer wall and the wall of an adjacent room. In this case you might like to fit a rope handrail.

Method

1   Fit the picture screws into the outside wall at the top and bottom of the staircase, at a suitable height above the stairs.

2   Thread the silk cord through the eyes of the screws, up the length of the staircase, finishing with a decorative loop at each end.

3   Stitch through the cord to secure firmly in place.

Materials

2 small gilt picture screws
Silk picture cord
Cotton thread

STAIRS ARE NOT ESSENTIAL

A basic staircase is fitted in most dolls' houses, but in a small two-room house, for example, is sometimes omitted to save space. In this case, you can give the impression that there is a staircase out of sight by fitting a non-opening door to the inside back wall. Paint the door before fitting, then simply glue it on to the wall, fairly near the corner of the room. To make this arrangement appear realistic, it is worth making a proper door surround.

▶ A non-opening door at the rear of this small dining room gives the impression of a hall beyond. The room has been made a more interesting shape by bringing part of the back wall forward to create a recess for the door To do this, glue a piece of MDF or polyboard about ¾in (20mm) thick to the back wall before decorating.

SIMPLE FLOORING

The simplest floor covering for a dolls' house is fitted carpet. As an attractive alternative, various types of fixed hard flooring may be used.

CARPET

Self-adhesive felt with peel-off backing is available in a limited colour range from dolls' house stockists and haberdashers, but you will have a wider choice if you use fine wool, woollen-mixture, or velvet dress fabrics. Very dark or very bright colours tend to swamp the contents of a room: a medium tone or simple pattern gives the best effect. Lay carpet when the decorating is complete and the skirting boards have been fitted, fixing it down with double-sided adhesive tape.

FIXED HARD FLOORING

Parquet floor for the sitting room, black and white tiles for the hall and quarry tiles or flagstones for the kitchen are all possibilities, and can be laid in a single piece. Sheets of fibreglass cladding representing these materials can be cut with a craft knife or scissors and glued directly on the wooden floors of the house using PVA white wood glue. Fit hard flooring before gluing skirting boards in place.

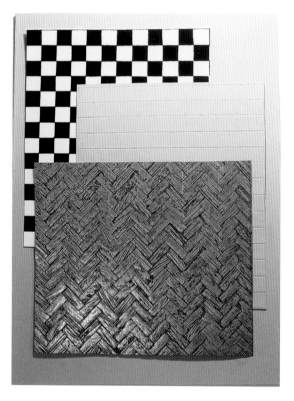

▲ Easy to apply fibreglass sheets make dealing with flooring a simple matter. Yellow quarry tiles, black-and-white tile effect and parquet flooring would be suitable for kitchen, hall and sitting room.

◄ The join between two different types of flooring in adjacent rooms can look untidy. Copy the method used in full-size houses and cover the join with thin brass strip, available from hobby shops. ICut to size using a small saw, and glue in place.

CUTTING FLOOR PATTERNS

The most fail-safe way to ensure that hard flooring fits perfectly is to cut a paper pattern first. This avoids unfortunate mistakes when cutting the sheets. If you keep the paper patterns they can save some fiddly measuring if you decide to refurbish at a later date. Use fairly stiff paper for the patterns. Uncreased brown or photocopy paper is ideal.

Method

1　Measure the room size and cut a piece of paper about 1in (25mm) larger all round than the finished size of the flooring.

2　Lay the paper on the floor of the room, with one edge along the front edge of the room. Crease the paper to fit the sides and back of the room before cutting; snip and fold at awkward corners to get a good fit. If there are tricky joins or alcoves, add an extra piece of paper and join with adhesive tape.

3　Trim the pattern carefully. Check that it fits exactly and make any final adjustments. Write 'top' and 'front' clearly on the pattern to avoid mistakes when using it to cut the flooring material itself.

PAPER FLOORS

Paper printed to simulate a variety of flooring materials is also available from dolls' house stockists, but it is not hard-wearing. A paper floor is a good temporary measure while you decide on something more permanent. Paper cut-outs of oriental carpets from magazines, for example, can look surprisingly effective on a dolls' house floor. Even brown paper can represent a wooden floor in a small room: use semi-matt kraft paper, the type which has small lines.

▲ Samples of suitable paper flooring materials.

REALISTIC FLOORS

If you want more realistic flooring in your dolls' house, using miniature versions of the real thing simply cannot be beaten. Real wooden planking, flagstones or Victorian-style tiles are individually made, so they are more expensive than sheet flooring. They also take time to fit, but are worth the effort involved for the effect they give.

The materials for this type of floor are more expensive and more time-consuming to install than sheet flooring, but will last as long as the house and should never need replacing. The time and trouble taken and the expense should be amply rewarded by the look of the finished room. Here are details of some more elaborate treatments:

PLANKED FLOORING

Ready-cut strips of iron-on oak, pine or mahogany veneer make realistic planked floors (see photograph on page 98). Dolls' house stockists sell packs of miniature planking in 18in (460mm) lengths with instructions; these hints should help to avoid pitfalls:

1 Cut a card pattern for the floor (see photograph). and use as a base on which to fix the planks. It is a good idea to paint the card using watercolour paint in a colour similar to that intended for the finished planking so that minute gaps between planks will not be obvious. The front edge of the card should also be coloured so that a white streak does not show when the floor is in place.

2 Cut the planking with scissors or a craft knife. The longest planks should be about three-quarters of the length of the room, staggered as on a real floor, and with short lengths used at the ends or as spacers. Try to keep the pieces in the order they were cut, so that when they are laid down and butted together there is a neat join between each.

3 For a Tudor house, leave unvarnished. For a Georgian or Shaker-style house, finish with one or two coats of matt varnish. For other periods, use two or even three coats of semi-matt varnish.

▲ Cutting a card pattern for a planked floor.

Direction of floorboards
Floorboards in a house normally run from front to back because the joists run across, between supporting walls at the side. In a dolls' house, however, the effect is better if the boards run parallel with the front. Start with one extra-long plank right across the front to give a clean edge.

VARNISHING PLANKING

Varnishing requires a slightly different technique from painting: the trick is to imagine that you are floating the varnish over the surface of the wood. I use a ¾in (19mm) brush, or ½in (12mm) for a very small house. A dust-free atmosphere is important while the surface is drying, because varnish seems to attract any small particles and these will spoil the finished effect. Varnish produces strong fumes, so work in a well-ventilated room, with the window open if possible.

1 Use light, smooth strokes, never dab at a spot you think you may have missed: wait for the next coat to cover it.

2 Rub down lightly between coats with the finest glasspaper.

3 For a really smooth finish, rub over gently with a soft cloth (not glasspaper) before applying the final coat.

FLAGSTONES

Ceramic or resin flagstones are ideal for the Tudor or Georgian home, especially for the kitchen (see page 94). They are thicker than sheet flooring (see page 88) and must be cut to fit awkward corners. Ceramic flagstones can be cut with a standard, tungsten-carbide-tipped tile cutter; follow the instructions on the pack carefully. Resin flagstones can be cut with a junior hacksaw.

Glue the flagstones on to a card base cut to the exact shape of the room or, if you are confident, directly to the wooden floor of the dolls' house. Use a latex-based adhesive for ceramic flagstones. Wood glue works best with resin ones, which will also be improved by a coat of satin-finish varnish in a light shade such as pine or light oak.

▲ To fit an external doorstep, measure, cut and paint a strip of wood and glue to the front of the house or between the edges of the door surround. Make sure the base is level with the base of the rest of the front, so that it does not catch when the house is opened. It should be thick enough to conceal any small gap which would otherwise show below the door.

Opening doors

Before you make a final decision on flooring material, check whether opening doors will allow for the extra thickness. This can be a problem with more realistic flooring options such as flagstones. If the door is likely to scrape along the flooring, or not open at all, unscrew the hinges and cut a thin strip off the base before refitting. With a front door, you may need to make an extra exterior doorstep to fill the resulting gap. Measure carefully and cut stripwood of a suitable thickness to make one or two steps as necessary – the steps shown are ⅜in (10mm) high. Paint the step an appropriate colour and glue in place at the base of the doorway.

FITTINGS

To add the finishing touches to your interior decoration, skirtings, cornices, door and window frames need to be fitted.

DOOR FRAMES

Whether or not you have chosen to fit interior doors, a door frame can give a finished appearance to an opening between rooms. It will also cover wallpaper edges or make a neat finish to emulsion paint round the doorway. All you need to do is cut three pieces of wood moulding, using the method for mitring corners on fireplace mouldings (see page 79). Paint the wood as required and glue in place around the door or opening. As an alternative to wood moulding, use braid trim to make a surround.

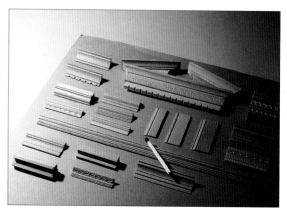

▲ Replica wooden mouldings provide accurate period detail in a Georgian, Victorian or modern room. The broken pediment can be used over a doorway or to top a bookcase (see page 120).

SKIRTINGS, CORNICES, DADO AND PICTURE RAILS

These fittings are optional, but have the advantage of concealing edges where, in the miniature scale, it would be difficult to make a perfect join. They are also historically correct for some period houses.

Scaled-down wooden mouldings suitable for these fittings are supplied in 18in (460mm) or occasionally 12in (305mm) lengths. When measuring, allow a little extra so that the ends of each piece can be mitred at the corners of the rooms and the edges of any chimney breasts.

It is worth buying an extra length to allow for mistakes and changes to plans during fitting. Left-over short lengths are useful for making up fireplaces (see pages 80–81).You might also want to practise cutting mitres on a spare piece.

All these fittings are best glued lightly with all-purpose adhesive rather than PVA wood glue. They need not be fixed permanently as you may wish to remove them later for redecoration.

> **Avoiding joins**
> Always use one complete piece of moulding along each wall. A join never looks satisfactory as it always shows when painted, however carefully it is sanded.

SKIRTINGS

Thin stripwood is economical for skirtings and can simply be butted together at the corners of the room. This method is also very suitable for children's dolls' houses (see page 52).

To fit scaled-down replicas of period-style skirtings, it is worth taking the trouble to learn how to cut a mitre for the joins. Most modern homes have skirting boards, so that you can check the real thing to see how the pieces fit together.

Many dolls' houses have internal doorways very close to the front of the house, so there will be a wall space of only about ½in (13mm) between the front opening edge of the house and the side of the door frame. In theory this gap should also have skirting fitted, but in practice such a small piece will look messy and it is best to omit it.

Mitred joins
The angle for cutting mitred joins is the same for skirtings, cornices, dado and picture rails (see method above), but different for fireplaces, door, window and picture frames (see page 79). You will find this easier if you compare the relative positions of the moulding on a skirting board and a fireplace.

Method

1 To cut a mitre in replica wooden moulding, place the plain back of the moulding upright against the back of the mitre box (see diagram), in the same position as it will be fitted against the wall in the house. Note that this position is different from that used when cutting moulding for fireplaces, door and window frames.

2 Cut the mouldings for the rear wall first and check the fit.

3 Next cut the pieces for each side wall. Cut the mitre first and, when you are sure that it fits, cut off the excess length at the front. Identify each piece in pencil on the reverse.

4 Paint or varnish as required and leave to dry thoroughly.

5 Glue in place.

Correct angle for cutting mitred corners in wood moulding for skirting boards

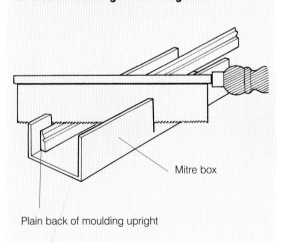

Mitre box

Plain back of moulding upright

CORNICES

Cornices were a standard fitting in rooms during the 18th and 19th centuries. A large, impressive cornice might have been used in the main rooms, and more modest ones in the bedrooms and service rooms. Prepare and fit as for skirtings. A wallpaper border can be used to define the top edge of the wall instead or in addition (see photograph below). Lace trimming is a pretty and simple alternative: just glue it in place.

PICTURE RAILS

You may want to fit picture rails in your dolls' house. In a room with a wall height of 10–11in (255–280mm), for example, the picture rail should be placed about 1½in (40mm) from the ceiling. Whatever the style of decoration on the walls, the area of wall above the picture rail should be coloured to match the ceiling.

DADO RAILS

A dado rail will help to give the correct appearance to a Georgian room, but is best omitted from a very small house in which it will create too many divisions. If present, it should be placed at about one-third of the height of the room (it was originally intended to be level with the back of an upright chair, to prevent it marking the wall). It can also mark a change in pattern or wall colour, with a plain surface below the rail and wallpaper above, or a dark colour below and a paler one above.

Keeping rails level

Not all dolls' house walls are exactly straight. The simplest way to fit a dado rail accurately is to decide its height above the floor and cut a rectangle of card the same length and about 2in (50mm) wide. Align the bottom of the card with the floor and move it round the room, using the top as a guide to pencil in lines. Check that the lines meet at the corners and that the height matches at the front. For a picture rail, use the same method but measure down from the ceiling. If the style of decoration is to be different above and below, the pencil line will indicate where to end wallpaper and begin emulsion paint. The rail can be glued on to conceal the join.

◀ A wallpaper border and dado rail add emphasis to this large room. The angle of cut for the dado and cornice to fit the corners of a chimney breast is exactly the opposite to that used in the corner of a room on these fittings. On the chimney breast the joins project outwards into the room instead of fitting together in a corner.

INTERNAL DOORS

Doors between rooms are not essential in a dolls' house and they are sometimes supplied as optional extras with both finished houses and kits. A simple archway or opening between the rooms has the advantage of making the house seem lighter and more spacious. You can fit internal doors yourself, but it is not the easiest of tasks unless you have some woodwork experience. Care is needed to make sure they are hung perfectly straight.

Another potential obstacle is that, if the hinges are to scale, the screws will be so tiny that dealing with them is extremely fiddly. If they are dropped, they may never be found. Manufacturers of dolls' house kits sometimes supply oversize hinges and screws, which are easier for the amateur to manage. The result is inevitably less elegant but more practical. It is a good idea to substitute smaller, neater brass hinges for those provided. Fix them in place with superglue. This gives a better effect, and means that large screwheads will not prevent the door from closing properly.

Keeping screws safe

Keep screws in an egg-cup while fitting hinges, and use tweezers to pick them up. 'Partpicker' tweezers with a magnifier attached may be helpful. Fit doorknobs before fixing the doors in place, so that the door can be laid flat.

Method

1 First check that the door is the right way up. On a four-panel door the longer panels go at the top; on a six-panel door the smallest panels go at the top. Plan to fit the door so that it opens into the room and away from the front of the house. This will make it easier to see through into the room on the other side of the door.

2 Make sure that the hinges are the right way round so that the door will open. Drill holes and screw the hinges on to the door first.

3 Holding the door in place, mark the position for the other side of the hinges on the door frame, then drill the holes and screw into place.

4 Paint or varnish the doors before fitting.

◀ In general, I am happy to omit internal doors in the interests of light. I also like the way in which, by looking through a doorway, different views of the rooms are opened up. I decided to fit internal doors in my interior design shop, however, as everything is arranged so that the displays look best from the front.

CLOTH HINGES

For a child's dolls' house, cloth hinges are ideal. They are not invisible, but are reasonably neat and serviceable. Children enjoy being able to open and shut doors to add realism to their games and cloth hinges are easily replaced if there are accidents.

Method

1 Cut a narrow strip of cotton tape or seam binding just shorter that the height of the door.

2 Fold the tape firmly and accurately in half lengthwise, and iron in the crease.

3 Using all-purpose adhesive, glue the folded tape first to the door edge and then to the edge of the door frame on one side of the aperture, just as for normal hinges (see diagram).

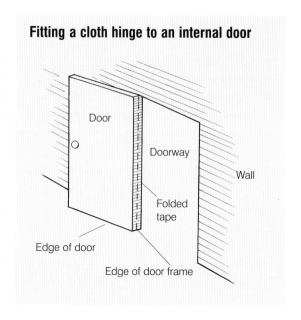

Fitting a cloth hinge to an internal door

Door

Doorway

Wall

Folded tape

Edge of door

Edge of door frame

SPECIAL FEATURES

Before getting down to details, you might like to consider building in a larger special feature. Depending on the style of your house, one or more of these suggestions may be suitable:

KITCHEN RANGE RECESS

A range is the focal point of any Victorian kitchen. It will look even more impressive if it is fitted into a recess, with a chimney breast above and a wide mantelshelf for displaying ornaments. A chimney breast the full width of the kitchen will provide useful storage space either side of the range for a coal scuttle and a kettle on a stand. The same method could be used to create a recess for an Aga cooker.

▲ The finished kitchen with its built-in range.

Method

1 Cut three lengths of the square dowelling, one to fit against each side wall, and one to go above them on top of the wall to make a frame for the recess.

2 Measure the depth of the range and glue dowelling to walls and ceiling ½in (13mm) further forward than this measurement.

3 Cut a piece of thick cardboard the width of the back wall and approximately 3½in (90mm) high. Glue to the top of the wooden surround so that it forms the chimney breast above the range.

4 Paint or wallpaper the card to match the intended decor of the rest of the room.

Materials

½in (13mm) square wooden dowelling
Thick cardboard
Wooden moulding (for mantelshelf and side trim)
Paint, wallpaper and/or tiles as required

5 Glue a piece of mantelshelf moulding to the front of the chimney breast at the base of the card, and a piece down each side over the dowelling. This can be stained or painted before gluing in place.

6 Paper the inside of the recess with fake tile paper, or use ceramic tiles for a more realistic effect.

7 Place the range and any ornaments or cooking utensils in the recess.

INGLENOOK FIREPLACE

The typical wide chimney breast over an open hearth in an old cottage or Tudor house is known as an inglenook, as there was sufficient space on each side of the fire to sit in the 'nook'. These fireplaces were constructed by incorporating a solid oak beam instead of a mantelshelf over the fireplace.

An inglenook fireplace can be made in the same way as the kitchen range recess. Instead of mantelshelf moulding, glue a piece of oak veneer about 1in (25mm) high to the front of the chimney breast. Before gluing in place, distress the wood slightly by denting it with a small hammer, and stain to resemble darkened oak. Line the fireplace with brick paper or brick cladding.

▲ This brick-lined inglenook fireplace boasts a traditional cast-iron fireback and a rotating spit as well as a pot crane and a hanging griddle tray. Horse brasses, a corn dolly and a bread dough harvest twist all add to the atmosphere of a well-used kitchen.

HALF-TIMBERING

Tudor-style dolls' houses are half-timbered on the outside, but the internal walls are usually supplied plain, whether the house is bought ready-made or as a kit. It is rare in a genuine Tudor house to find that all the rooms have been plastered over, so it is a good idea to add some internal timbers to complement those on the outside. You might want to leave one or two rooms – perhaps the parlour and a bedroom – without timbering, and decorate these with a stencil design (see page 106).

Use thin stripwood (available from hobby shops) and dent it by knocking with a small hammer. Cut the strips slightly crooked: straight edges will look unnatural. In reality such timbers are part of the framework of the house and therefore as thick inside as out, but I find it is better to scale the size down a little for the interior so the effect does not look overdone in such a small space. The main timbers might be ½in (12mm) or ⅝in (15mm) wide and the infill timbers ¼in (6mm) or ⅜in (10mm) wide, but the proportions will vary to suit your house: make them in whatever width looks best. Satin-finish or varnish the timbers to resemble oak before fixing in place with all-purpose glue.

The patterns made by timbering on plain walls are even more effective if you plan in advance where to display large pieces of furniture and paintings, because you can site the timbering to suit your needs perfectly. I always base internal half-timbering on photographs of real examples. Look at pictures in books or magazines if you cannot see originals.

▲ Crooked beams make a surround for an original miniature oil painting. The planked floor in undarkened oak helps keep the room light.

Staining beams and panelling
Use light oak stain if you want to give the impression that the house is newly-built. Medium oak stain makes a pleasing contrast against plain walls and is my choice. Use dark oak stain if you want the house to look as though it is 400 years old and has darkened with age. In a Georgian house, use a genuine Georgian paint colour. Choose a sample from a range of historic paint colours – these are produced by a number of manufacturers.

WOOD PANELLING

Wood-panelled rooms are an attractive feature. In a late Tudor dolls' house they give a realistic feel, and should be stained to resemble oak. Plain panelling also suits an early Georgian house, in which it would have been painted, not stained.

Method

1   Cut veneer or thin ply to fit the space that is to be panelled.

2   Cut a length of stripwood to fit along the base and a similar piece for the top of the panelling.

3   Mark out the placing for the uprights at approximately ¾in (20mm) intervals. This can vary a little as they need not be spaced regularly.

4   Cut an upright to the required height, using a mitre block with a straight slot. This will ensure that the cut is straight at top and bottom, to create a neat fit against the cross-pieces. Mark this first upright and keep it to use as a guide to cut all the others to the same length. Do not use the guide piece, as the others will be fractionally longer when cut.

5   Stain all the wood before gluing on: if there are any minute smudges of glue, woodstain will not cover them and they will show up as bare patches later.

▲ Plain oak panelling with plastered (painted) walls above. In this case the uprights and crosspieces are fitted over oak veneer, but a similar effect can be achieved by using inexpensive wood and distressing and staining it before gluing in place.

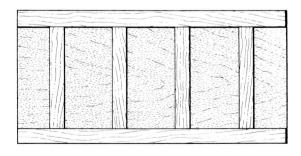

◀ A section of veneer or thin ply overlaid with stripwood to create panelling.

9

Interior decoration

When you have fitted any interior features you want, it is time to think about decoration. You may choose the simple approach, with painted walls and basic flooring, or you may have more ambitious plans. Here are some ideas and techniques that should inspire you.

EMULSION PAINT

This is the quickest and easiest way to decorate interior walls. Cover floors before you begin and always apply two coats of paint to avoid any patchiness showing up later. Undercoat and paint door and window frames before fitting them if possible. If they are already fitted, paint them before decorating the walls. Start at the back wall and work forwards, to avoid smudging a newly-painted area with the back of your hand.

◀ Painting a narrow stairwell is an awkward business, and care must be taken to achieve a smooth covering of paint.

STAIRWELLS

Fixed stairs make decorating more difficult, especially if they are narrow, steep and enclosed. The easiest way to paint a very narrow upper hall is to do as much with a brush as can be reached conveniently (see photograph). Then paint the less-accessible area on the side and back walls using a small sponge attached to a paint stick with a rubber band. Take care not to over-saturate the sponge, and cover the stairs with masking tape to avoid splashes while painting. Balusters and handrails can also be protected with paper or masking tape. Work in a good light so you can see exactly what you are doing. An angled or desk light will help you to see properly into the back corners. A torch makes a good temporary spotlight.

With fixed-in stairs, the zigzag shape where the treads meet the wall can be a problem. Rule a line on the wall down the side of the stairs and finish the emulsion paint above it (see photograph opposite). Paint or varnish below the line to match the stair treads and/or skirting boards, then glue on a strip of beading to cover the line itself.

▶ Thin beading will cover the join between the edge of the treads and the emulsion above.

Paintbrushes

Do not throw away old art paintbrushes. Cut off the brush end and use the wooden part as a useful paint stick for stirring paints and decorating awkward areas such as stairwells.

WALLPAPER

Dolls' house wallpaper is supplied in separate pieces rather than on a roll. Allow one piece for each wall. It is wise to buy an extra sheet to allow for pattern repeats or wastage. Measure all the walls before you go shopping, and remember to allow for chimney breasts and doorways, which may involve joins.

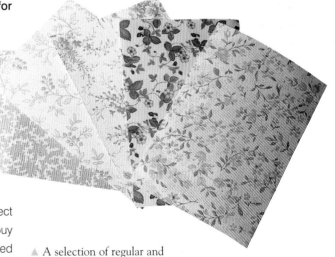

Ordinary gift wrap is cheaper than specially-made wallpaper and comes in far larger sheets. It is worth looking in the stationer's, as occasionally you will find the perfect design. I would still recommend that you should buy an extra sheet in case of accidents. If it is not needed for the dolls' house, you can always use it for wrapping up presents!

▲ A selection of regular and miniaturised wallpapers. It is difficult to tell by appearance alone which is which. Regular wallpaper is thicker and will not stretch when pasted. Remnants of patterned wallpaper can be useful: use part of the design for the walls and create a complementary border, perhaps from a strip. Piecing is not difficult in such a small scale.

USING A PAPER PATTERN

As with fixed hard flooring (see page 89), you will find it easier to cut a paper pattern before cutting the wallpaper itself. Use fairly stiff paper and cut a separate pattern for each wall. The pattern for each side wall should extend by about ⅛in (3mm) to fit around the corner and on to the back wall. Paper the side walls first then fit the back, cut exactly to size, neatly over to make an almost-invisible join and avoid the possibility of a gap. If the edges are to be concealed behind skirtings, cornices or borders, the paper need not fit exactly to the top and bottom of the walls.

If you need to fit paper round a door that is situated near a corner, it is best to make the join at the top of the door. A separate piece can then be used for the small area above and to the side of the door (see diagram). If you try to hang a piece for the whole wall, there is a risk of tearing the fragile strip of paper . If you have fitted a chimney breast, plan a join on either side.

The best way to paper between a door and the wall

Join

Front edge of house

Doorway   *Wall*

When you cut out the wallpaper pieces from your patterns, make sure that the design is the right way up and that any repeat pattern will match at the joins, allowing for the ⅛in (3mm) overlap at the back corners. To avoid mistakes, pencil 'left', 'right' and 'back' lightly on the reverse of the appropriate piece before applying it.

OPENING FRONTS

Covering the inside of the opening front is trickier than papering a room, as you will need to omit the windows and doorways. The easiest way to do it is to paper straight over them. Wait until the next day, when the paper has dried thoroughly, then cut carefully round the edges of each aperture using a craft knife.

For the opening front of a small house, one piece of paper will be sufficient. You could use a different paper for each floor, but the effect is likely to be more attractive if you choose a single design that complements all the interior decorations.If you need to join sheets of paper, try to place the join at the edge of a window, where it will be less noticeable.

▲ The opening front of my interior design shop was almost twice the depth of the wallpaper I chose, so I used a strategically-placed wallpaper border to attract attention to the window display and disguise the join.

PAPERHANGING

Hanging wallpaper in a dolls' house is far easier than in full-sized rooms, but care is still needed, particularly if you are using special 1/12-scale paper. The important thing is to take your time: make sure that you are placing the wallpaper accurately, and take care to avoid depositing stray smears of paste.

Method

1 Mix some regular wallpaper paste according to the maker's instructions. If you are using 1/12-scale paper, you will need to make the paste slightly thinner.

2 Size (prepare) the walls first by pasting over them, and leave to dry for about 30 minutes or until dry to the touch.

3 Paste each piece of wallpaper immediately before hanging, making sure that the paste reaches right to the edges. Hang the side walls first and the back wall last.

4 For each side wall, line up the front edge first, to avoid the need to trim later. Smooth the paper over the whole wall, then press gently all over with screwed-up soft paper. Use a fresh piece for each wall to avoid accidental trails of paste.

5 Do not panic if your newly applied wallpaper seems full of bubbles and lumps: this is part of thedrying-out process. Save left-over paste until the next day. If any corners or front edges have not adhered properly, stick them down by working the paste under the edge using a small brush.

▲ A wallpaper with a plain border has been fitted instead of curtains or blinds to emphasize the windows and the floor divisions inside a three-storey 18th-century house.

Applying wallpaper

Some wallpapers that have been specially designed in 1/12 scale are very thin, and will stretch alarmingly if over-wetted. The thicker the paper, the easier it is to paste up. It is also worth looking at regular wallpapers with small patterns.

STAIRCASES AND HALLS

It is not easy to paper round a fixed-in staircase, especially if it has a half-landing and a second flight of stairs leading from the back. If you are sure you want wallpaper rather than emulsion paint, choose a pattern that does not need matching. A marbled or mottled effect will be easier to fit. I used a large sheet of hand-marbled paper for the staircase in my eighteenth-century shop (see right). It was even thicker than regular wallpaper, so I could slide it along awkward angles without any risk of tearing.

Using marble-effect paper solves another potential difficulty. The base of the wall at the back of a half-landing is almost inaccessible, and fitting skirtings is virtually impossible. With a marble wall, skirting boards are not strictly necessary, and I prefer the simpler effect when the 'marble' joins the floor with no adornment.

Fit the wallpaper against the staircase edge on the side wall using the method for painting the same area see page 100). The wallpaper should finish above the pencil line. Paint or varnish below the line as appropriate, and add a strip of beading along the join.

▲ In the 18th century, wallpaper painted to simulate expensive marble became popular. If the paper is chosen carefully it can look impressive, but may be too ostentatious for the smaller home. In a large house or a shop it is ideal.

WALLPAPER BORDERS

A pretty border along the top of a plain wall will make a neat finish and is equally effective whether used with a plain wallpaper or over emulsion paint. Scaled-down designs are available to complement 1/12-scale wallpapers. It is worth investigating other sources for suitable borders, from advertising leaflets to full-size wallpaper borders, where part of the pattern can be selected for miniature use by judicious cutting.

Borders can be used with or instead of cornices. They can also be used instead of wood as an attractive frame for a door or window, or in place of a wooden dado or picture rail.

▲ A selection of borders to enhance plain walls:: one is cut out from a supermarket leaflet, while the others include a 1/12-scale border and two trimmed from regular wallpaper borders. They can also be used to surround doors or windows, or in place of a dado rail.

Method

1 Cut a separate length of border for each wall, making sure the pattern will match where it is to be joined at or near the corners. It is best to butt the pieces together with no overlap.

2 Paste one length at a time, wait for a minute and then apply. Do the side walls first, lining up the front edge carefully to avoid the need to trim later.

3 Take care when applying the pasted length of border to the decorated wall: do not allow one end to trail, but press gently along the length using one hand and keep the paper under control with the other hand.

4 Press carefully with screwed-up kitchen paper as in the method for papering walls (see page 103).

Trimming edges
If excess wallpaper needs trimming from the front edges of walls, wait until it is thoroughly dry (preferably overnight) and then cut it with a sharp craft knife.

PAINT EFFECTS

If you enjoy playing with colour and have a bit of imagination, it is possible to create stunning effects. You need not stick to the colours on paint charts, but can mix and match until you have the result you want. Be adventurous in mixing different kinds of paint: some of the most interesting tones and finishes are achieved by mixing emulsion with gouache or model enamel. Professional interior decorators are fond of rag-rolling, stencilling and sponging, and these finishes are equally effective in 1/12 scale, both for interior and exterior use. The techniques below are examples of what can be done. They may well inspire other ideas.

▲ Whether the stencilling is real or, as in this case, fake – part of a wallpaper design has been used – emphasize the design by placing the decorative border above a picture rail.

STENCILLING

Stencilling has been popular in real houses for some years, and a plain wall can be brightened enormously by the judicious use of stencilled designs. In the miniature scale, it is best to keep such decoration to a minimum, because too much stencilling will look far too busy. A border round the room, or a simple design on just one wall will give the best effect.

Cutting out your own stencils in 1/12 scale is tricky unless you are unusually dextrous with small tools and have unlimited patience. I recommend using a ready-made miniature brass stencil. Fix the stencil with removable tape and colouring in, using a small paintbrush and stencil paints (also available in tiny sizes for miniaturists).

You can cheat by using sections of wallpaper border to achieve a similar effect. A running design (see photograph above) makes a good border.

CRAYONS

Waterproof pencil crayons (available from art shops) can be used for stencilling as an easy and less messy alternative to paint. There is a wide range of soft, pastel colours and the appearance of the finished design will look just as good. Sharpen the crayons frequently as a blunt tip will not reach into the corners of a tiny stencil design.

Paint pots

Plastic yoghurt pots are ideal for paint mixing: they are deep enough to allow vigorous stirring without splashing. If you want to keep the paint mix for a day or two, cover the pot with plastic food wrap to exclude air.

MARBLING

A painted marble effect is a more interesting alternative to marbled paper for small decorative items, a table top, or fireplace inset. If your house is grand enough to have pillars in the entrance hall, they can also be marbled using this method.

It is best to work with a picture of real marble in front of you as an example. You will probably want to try a few practice pieces first to get the hang of the technique. A delicately-veined marble will look most realistic, so take care not to be too heavy-handed with the paintbrush. You will need model enamel in your chosen colours, and a very fine brush. For the urn shown I used a base coat of cream model enamel. The veining was lightly painted in (feathered) using mid-green and yellow. For the lighter patches, the green was mixed with cream.

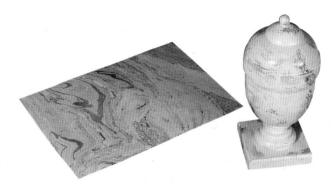

▲ It took only a few minutes to transform a plain, turned wooden urn by painting it to resemble marble.

SILVER-BLUE EFFECT

'Gustavian-style' furniture, which first became popular in 18th-century Sweden, seems to be enjoying something of a revival. It will add a touch of glamour to a 1/12-scale period room, just as it will to an ultra-modern interior.

Paint simple, plain furniture using the method for creating a verdigris effect (see page 117), but using silver (metallic) model enamel instead of bronze. To alter the appearance of the plain X-frame stool, pale blue emulsion was mixed first with dark blue model enamel to make mix A, and then with pale blue to make mix B.

▲ The top of the repainted X-frame stool is covered with blue-and-white striped cotton and trimmed with narrow braid in a complementary colour, in the approved Swedish fashion.

10
Soft furnishings

No house is complete without something for its residents to sit on. There are any number of kits available, offering all kinds of seating, but it can be fun to supplement these with a few home-made and comfortable-looking items. Here are a few ideas that should inspire you.

SIMPLE CHAIR

Professionally-made wooden chairs are expensive, as they require expertise, time and patience to construct. This simple upholstered chair is armless, and requires no woodworking skills to complete.

Materials

Cube of balsawood, approximately 1⅛in (40mm) across
Two pieces of thick cardboard, each 1½ x 3in (38 x 75mm)
Dressmaker's wadding
Cotton fabric (or curtain trimming), minimum width 3in (75mm)
Thin braid or silk cord (optional)

Checks
If you choose check fabric as your chair covering, take care to match the checks accurately at the joins.

▲ The red check material is actually a wide ribbon, while the patterned covering is part of some curtain border trim.

Method

1 Fold one piece of cardboard in half so that it measures 1½in by 1½in (40 x 40mm). Glue to the back of the balsawood block, with the folded edge at the top. Tape round both the cardboard and the block with adhesive tape for extra strength (see diagram 1). This gives extra thickness at the back of the seat, so that when it is glued on, it will slope slightly backwards instead of being bolt upright.

2 Cut two pieces of fabric 3 x 6½n (75 x 165mm). Fold each piece in half lengthwise and press.

3 Glue one piece round the balsawood base (the seat) with the fold at the top, joining centre back with an overlap (see diagram 2).

4 Glue the second piece of fabric over the balsawood base, with the folded edge at the front, joining underneath with an overlap at the centre of the base (see diagram 3). Make sure that this piece neatly covers the top of the first piece of fabric at the front.

5 Cut a piece of wadding 3 x 3in (75 x 75mm). Fold and glue this over the second piece of cardboard with the fold at one side and the edges meeting at the other (see diagram 4) to form the chair back.

6 Cut a piece of fabric 2½in (60mm) wide by 6in (152mm) long and fold over the padded chair back with the fold going over the top and the raw edges at the bottom (see diagram 5). Turn in the edges neatly and sew down each side.

7 Glue the chair back to the back of the seat (see diagram 6).

8 As an optional extra, sew on some very thin silk cord or braid round the edges to trim.

Constructing a simple covered chair

1 Tape right round wood and cardboard. Folded card glued to wood

2 Wrap fabric round block, joining at centre back

3 Wrap second piece of fabric over block, joining underneath

4 Fold wadding round card

5 Fold. Wrap fabric over the padded card and sew round edges

6 Glue back to the seat block

SOFA

This simple armless sofa is based on corrugated card packaging. The base and the back and seat cushions can be covered in the type of plasticated paper flower wrap that has a faint self-pattern and a slight sheen. It has the added attraction of being free when you buy a bunch of flowers! It is strong, easy to cut, and will look like fabric when the sofa is finished. My sofa is 3½in (90mm) long, 1½in (40mm) deep and about 2⅜in (60mm) high, but dimensions can be altered to suit your room.

▲ This armless sofa is perfect for a modern room. Red cushions made from non-fray seam binding and a striking black and white rug complete the effect.

Method

1   Fold the corrugated paper packaging over several times to a thickness of approximately ⅝in (16mm), and tape together securely. Make the back and seat cushions using the same packaging. The back should be about ⅜in (10mm) thick and the seat and back cushions about ¼in (6mm) thick.

2   Cover the sofa with two or more thicknesses of flower wrap so that the base box or corrugated paper shape do not show through. First, cut a strip of paper long enough to fold around from end to end of the base. Fix it in place with double-sided tape. Then cut and fold another strip of paper to fold around the base from front to back, over the first strip. Fix this underneath the sofa.

3   Cover the back, seat cushion and two smaller back cushions in the same way.

4   Cut a piece of plain card to make a support for the back. Fold it in half and fix to the base back and underneath. Cover with flower-wrap. Fix the back and seat cushions in place, then add the two small back cushions.

POUFFE

A pouffe is a padded, comfortable variation on a basic wooden stool and can be used either as extra seating or as a footstool. A 1930s or 1940s house would not be complete without one.

Method

1 Cut two pieces of fabric:
   (a) a circle about ⅜in (10mm) larger all round than the top of the foam rubber;
   (b) a rectangle the same height as the foam rubber and long enough to go round it, allowing an extra ⅜in (10mm) as an overlap.

2 Snip the circle of fabric at intervals, making the cuts no more than ¼in (6mm) long. Apply a thin trail of all-purpose glue round the edge and attach the fabric to the top of the foam rubber, bending over the side edges where snipped, to give a neat fit (see diagram 1).

3 Apply the glue to the edges of the rectangle of fabric and attach round the sides of the foam rubber, covering the snipped edges at the top (see diagram 1).

4 Cut braid the same length as the rectangle of fabric and glue round the sides to cover the join at the top.

5 Use a strong needle and thread (with a thimble) to go right through from underneath to the top of the pouffe. Take the thread back down and pull tight to create an indentation in the top (see diagram 2). Secure firmly with a knot at the base. Sew a small bead in the centre of the top to finish.

Materials

Cylindrical piece of foam rubber, about 1in (25mm) tall by 1¼in (30mm) in diameter (I found a piece in a bottle of bath salts; an alternative is a section of a large cork)
Fabric of your choice (perhaps a thick cotton)
Furnishing braid to trim
1 small bead

Making a pouffe

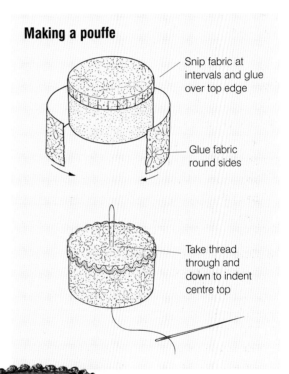

Snip fabric at intervals and glue over top edge

Glue fabric round sides

Take thread through and down to indent centre top

◀ The fabric covering for my pouffe is a thick cotton. Narrower braid would have been more accurately to scale, but I decided to use a scrap I had as I liked the flamboyant effect. For a modern room, a leather-covered pouffe would be appropriate, and an old glove could be recycled to make the covering.

TABLES

Beautiful tables can be made from kits, but sometimes it is good to soften the appearance of a room with a covered or draped table. Here are two different possibilities.

ROUND COVERED TABLE

An economical way to create a round occasional table is to use a cotton reel base. The fabric covering it is the important part: no one will see what is underneath. This method disguises the cotton reel perfectly and prevents the fabric from sticking out at an awkward angle. A very thin fabric looks just right if it flares out a little; narrow braid can be glued round the lower edge of thicker fabric to weigh it down.

Materials

Plastic or wooden cotton reel
Firm card
Dressmaker's lightweight iron-on interlining
Fine fabric of your choice
Narrow braid (optional)

Method

1 Cut a circle from the card, approximately 2½in (65mm) in diameter. A jam jar lid will provide a suitably-sized pattern. Glue to the top of the cotton reel, matching the centres (see diagram 1).

2 Cut a circle of fabric measuring 2½in (65mm), plus twice the height of the table in diameter. A saucer or small plate might provide a pattern, or you could use a compass.

▲ For the cloth on this table I used an embroidered mat, one of a set bought at a jumble sale. In a Victorian room, a deep red or green woollen fabric would look well. Blue-and-white check gingham would suit a modern setting.

3 Cut a circle of interlining the same size as the card for the table top.

4 Match the centre of the fabric circle to the centre of the interlining circle and iron on (see diagram 2).

5 Mark the centre of the cloth with a pin and attach to the table top with double-sided adhesive tape or glue. The interlining will prevent either tape or glue showing through the cloth.

6 Spray the cloth with water until really damp, fit a rubber band round the sides and leave until completely dry to ensure that the cloth hangs in neat folds (see diagram 3).

7 If you wish, glue thin braid round the bottom of the cloth as a weight.

A round table based on a cotton reel

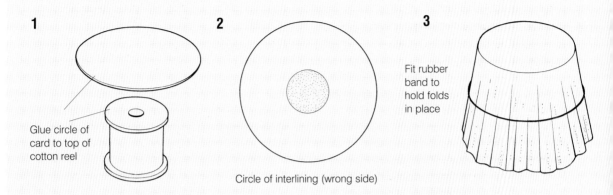

1 Glue circle of card to top of cotton reel

2 Circle of interlining (wrong side)

3 Fit rubber band to hold folds in place

DRAPED DRESSING TABLE

Country house dressing tables have been draped in this way for two centuries but have never gone out of fashion. It is a good way to make a pretty dressing table at minimal cost. Use lace for an elaborate effect, or sprigged cotton for a country cottage. Dimensions given are a guide. There is no standard size and measurements can be adapted to suit your room.

Materials

Block of wood (painted if necessary) or rigid box – suggested dimensions: 4in (100mm) long, 2½in (65mm) tall, 1¾in (45mm) deep
Piece of thin wood, or strong card approximately 5in (125mm) tall and 4in (100mm) long
Fake mirror glass or small handbag mirror
Acetate
Lace, or thin cotton fabric
Ribbon trimming (optional)
Coloured card (optional)

▲ The box used as the base for my dressing-table had a good finish so I left it as it was; wood should be painted before assembly if the top is not to be covered.

Method

1   Glue the thin wood or card to the back of the base (the wood block or box), so that the top half extends above the base to form a back for the mirror (see diagram and steps over the page).

2 Cut a piece of 'mirror' to fit using scissors, then glue to the backing card above the table top. If you use a tiny real mirror, you may need to adjust the measurements of the backing card; it can be narrower than the actual dressing table.

3 Cut a lace or cotton overskirt about 3in (75mm) high and 12in (305mm) long. Turn under ½in (12mm) along the top and tack or press in place. Gather the top edge to fit around the front and sides of the table. Arrange the gathers neatly, dab glue along the top and attach around the table.

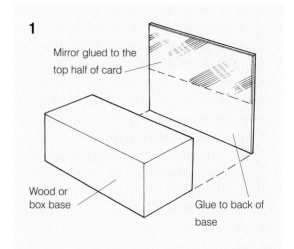

Mirror glued to the top half of card

Wood or box base

Glue to back of base

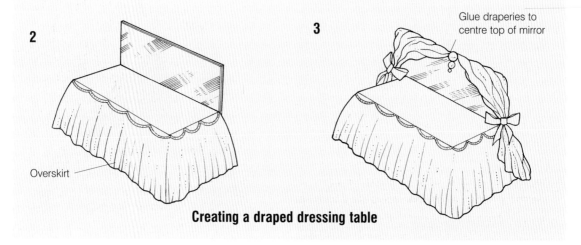

2 Overskirt

3 Glue draperies to centre top of mirror

Creating a draped dressing table

PEG DOLLS

The techniques of dressing a peg doll are not too dissimilar from those involved in the previous projects. Peg dolls are ideal for children's dolls' houses but, suitably dressed, can equally well inhabit the more rarefied atmosphere of a collector's 1/12-scale house.

▶ This peg doll is dressed as an 18th-century nursemaid. Bows of narrow satin ribbon add a delicate finishing touch to the lacy drapes of the cradle.

Method

1 For a stand-up doll, saw off the rounded tips of the peg to make a straight base. For a sit-down doll, saw off the lower part of the peg (see diagram 1).

2 Wind a pipe cleaner round the body and twist together firmly at centre back, fixing with a dab of glue. Tape round for extra security. Push the ends outwards to form the arms (see diagram 2).

3 For a sit-down doll, add a second pipe cleaner in the same way, at the base of the sawn-off peg, to form legs which can bend (see diagram 2).

4 Over-elaborate facial features can destroy the appeal of an otherwise charming doll: keep them simple. Use a fine line black pen and sketch on the eyes and mouth with two dots for a nose.

5 Make the hair in whatever style you want from the wool or thread, and glue in place.

6 To dress the doll, wrap a triangular piece of material or lace over the shoulders like a shawl to form the bodice and sleeves all in one piece (see diagram 3). Stitch under the arms to make the sleeves and secure the material back and front at the waist with a dab of glue. Add a gathered skirt and a ribbon sash to cover the join. A tiny hat or cap can be made from a scrap of lace edging.

Materials

Old-fashioned wooden clothes pegs with rounded tops
Pipe cleaners
Scraps of fabric and lace trim
Embroidery thread, stranded cotton or tapestry wool

Making stand-up and sit-down peg dolls

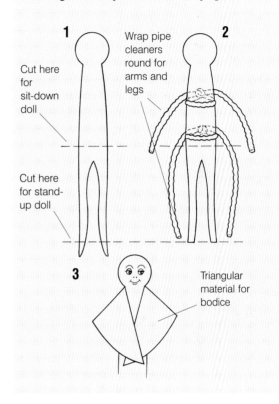

1 Cut here for sit-down doll
Cut here for stand-up doll
Wrap pipe cleaners round for arms and legs

2

3 Triangular material for bodice

Drawing faces

It is best to draw the face first before you add hair, so that if you are not happy with your first attempt, you can try again on the other side and cover up your mistake.

METAL KITS

The peg doll is shown with a professionally-made metal cradle. Metal is sometimes also used for kits, especially for small accessories with parts so tiny or intricate that it would not be possible to make them in wood, for example fireplace grates. Here are a few practical tips for their assembly.

Metal kits for small accessories are inexpensive, but are sometimes supplied without instructions. It can be daunting to be faced with a pile of unidentified bits of metal when you open the pack. There will be a picture of the finished miniature, however, and with patience you can work out from this how it all fits together. If possible, have a 'dry run' before gluing anything.

For an intricate kit where several different paint colours are to be used, it is worth investing in a magnifying glass (available from opticians or haberdashery departments) which can be hung around the neck on a cord, so that detailing will be 100% accurate.
A magnifier on a stand is even better and easier to use, and will have many other uses for the miniaturist.

Method

1 Smooth down the parts before assembly and remove all nobbles with a file. Roughen the places that are to be joined slightly before applying epoxy resin adhesive.

2 Paint with primer or undercoat and finish with model enamel, followed by a coat of clear varnish.

▶ The head of a girl was painted using the method below, but with a greenish-brown first coat rather than dark-brown.

BRONZE EFFECT

Classical statues and busts made in pewter or white metal are widely available and generally inexpensive. They can be transformed to look like bronze. This simple method also works well on plastic or ceramic.

Method

1 Paint with one coat of dark brown model enamel.

2 Apply a top coat of bronze metallic model enamel, rubbing off here and there with a rag before it dries, to reveal small patches of the duller brown.

3 When dry, buff with a dry soft cloth.

▶ A pewter bust of Napoleon looks impressive repainted as bronze and displayed on a mineral sample pedestal.

VERDIGRIS

A verdigris finish, to resemble the patina on old copper, brass or bronze, adds antique character to miniature urns, tubs and garden statues. Miniature terracotta pots provide a good base as paint dries in minutes on this material and you need not wait between stages. The same paint mix can be used on the roof of a garden building or the canopy over the balcony of a Regency house.

▲ Work in progress: three stages in achieving a verdigris finish on metal and terracotta.

Method

1 Apply a base coat of the pale blue emulsion to your chosen miniature pot.

2 Once the base coat is dry, apply a coat of bronze model enamel, making sure that it covers any ornamentation thoroughly.

3 Mix two different blue-green shades. Stir each thoroughly and try it out on paper. Adjust the proportions if necessary until Mix A is a bright, greeny-turquoise, and Mix B is paler than Mix A.

Mix A (dark)
1 dessertspoon of pale blue emulsion
A few drops each of lime green, deep blue, and mid-blue model enamel

◀ The finished urn looks very different from the original terracotta, with a patina resembling weathered bronze.

Materials

1 sample pot of pale blue emulsion
1 small can of model enamel in each of the following:
deep blue, lime green, mid-blue and metallic bronze.

Mix B (light)
1 dessertspoon of pale blue emulsion
A few drops each of mid-blue and lime green model enamel

4 Paint Mix A over the bronze, rubbing off with a paper kitchen towel so that the bronze shows through patchily.

5 Check that the paint is dry, then paint over some parts of the piece with Mix B, again partly rubbing off so that varying degrees of bronze and Mix A show through.

11
Furniture

There is a huge variety of furniture with which to fill your dolls' house. You may wish to collect professionally crafted 1/12-scale miniatures, or you may be happy with less expensive and plainer ready-made furniture. If you wish to save money, making your own furniture adds a personal touch and need not be complicated. You can use inexpensive materials that you may already have around the house. For the beginner, there are many excelllent kits available in a wide choice of styles, and these are a good starting point. This section offers advice on assembling kits and instructions for simple items of furniture. Making these pieces will give you an idea of what can be done without previous experience. As your skills in working with minuscule components improve, you can try making more sophisticated pieces.

▲ This simple kit is suitable for a beginner. The pieces are laser-cut and fit so well that glue is almost unecessary. This version of a Lutyens garden seat is made from MDF and can be spray-painted, but is also available in cherry or spruce, which can be polished or varnished.

KIT FURNITURE

Assembling a piece from a kit is the best way to begin. Wooden kits are designed by professionals to be made by the amateur and are not intended to be a test of skill. If you cannot understand the instructions, however, it may seem like one!

A picture of the finished piece can help you check that proportions are correct for the style, but not all kits include one. If there is no picture, see-through packs should enable you to check whether the wood is suitable for the design. The number of pieces is a guide to the level of ability required. The hints opposite may not appear in the manufacturer's instructions, but should help you to avoid frustration. It is a pity to spend time carefully assembling a kit, only to spoil it in the later stages.

◀ A kit set of Tudor table and benches on good-quality oak, shown part-assembled.

▼ The completed set, and a matching high-backed chair, has been stained with medium oak wood stain and polished for an authentic look.

Method

1 Check the parts by laying them out on a tray and making sure every piece is there. If you are not careful very tiny parts can easily fall out and be lost. It is a good idea to clear both the working surface and the surrounding area before you open the pack, so you can spot that tiny piece of wood or metal which might otherwise never be found again.

2 Read the instructions to familiarise yourself with the parts and the order in which they must be assembled. You may not be able to follow the complete sequence immediately. Read the first steps until you understand how the parts fit together and do not go on to the next stage until you have done this. The details should fall into place as you work.

3 Use the correct adhesive. Most kits specify the type if it is not supplied, and say whether components should be painted or varnished before or after assembly. If you leave surplus glue on wood, you will not be able to varnish or polish over it later. Keep white spirit handy and wipe off any tiny spots from the surface immediately. It is also useful for removing glue from fingers.

4 Use masking tape rather than clamps or rubber bands to keep small pieces together while glue is setting, and it peels off easily. Wind tape round an empty cotton reel and re-use several times.

5 When the instructions say 'keep square', make sure that you do. Find a small box around or into which you can fit the piece or, failing that, make a stiff cardboard shape to use as a mould, checking with a set square that the corners are accurate.

6 If the instructions say 'allow to dry and set' before the next stage, do so, or you may risk pushing the piece out of alignment or damaging it.

7 Rub over with fine glasspaper and wipe clean before polishing, painting or varnishing.

MAKING FURNITURE

When you have gained experience by assembling a few pieces of wooden furniture from kits, you may like to try making something of your own. The materials needed for these simple projects are inexpensive and easy to find. There are also ideas and instructions for making a variety of other pieces of furniture, none requiring complicated techniques or costly materials.

SIMPLE SHELVES

I made the shelves shown to fit a specific space in a room in my interior design shop but you can use this method to make any size. Leave them plain, or add decoration. I added an elaborate broken pediment from a kit to make them look more impressive. The shelves should be painted after assembly; varnishing should be done before gluing the parts together.

▲ The shelves are spaced to accommodate a collection of miniature glass of different sizes.

Method

1 Measure stripwood to the height required for the shelves and cut one piece for each side.

2 Decide on the number and width of the shelves required and cut these from stripwood. Measure carefully: these pieces will fit between the upright.

3 Cut one piece of stripwood for the top and one piece for the base of the shelves. These pieces will be glued on later to cover the ends of the uprights so they must be slightly longer than the shelves.

4 Cut shelf supports from matchsticks (or very thin stripwood). Measure the spaces carefully and glue at intervals down one side of each upright. Check that they are spaced identically on both sides, or your shelves will not be straight.

Materials

Plain stripwood, ½in (12mm) wide
Matchsticks
Wood moulding (optional)
Broken pediment kit (optional)

5 Glue the shelves on top of the supports, securely butted up against the uprights on either side. Finally glue on the top and base.

6 For extra decoration if desired, finish the base and sides with wood moulding and the top with a pediment.

Fitting the bookshelf components together.

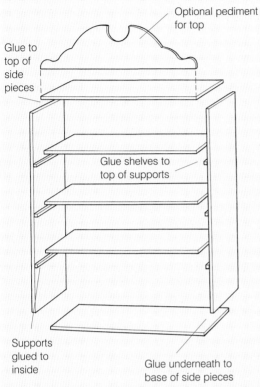

Optional pediment for top

Glue to top of side pieces

Glue shelves to top of supports

Supports glued to inside

Glue underneath to base of side pieces

▲ A good copy of a well-proportioned early 19th-century Biedermeier sofa, from a large range of European furniture mass-produced by a US manufacturer specialising in kits.

▲ Victorian-style kitchen furniture could also be used in a modern kitchen, depending on the finish. The shelf unit has been given a distressed look using an acrylic paint, and the chairs have been painted with a cheerful yellow Vincent Van Gogh might have enjoyed. For a Victorian kitchen, the furniture could be stained and then polished or varnished.

Cutting identical shelf lengths

To measure identical lengths of wood for shelves, cut a pattern from stiff card to the required length. Use as a guide when cutting each shelf. Do not cut the first shelf, then use it to mark out the others. Even the width of a thin pencil line will affect the measurement. Cut exactly on the pencil mark each time.

AGA COOKER

This single-oven Aga for a small kitchen is based on a wood block. It is not hard to make and the finished cooker will look solid and satisfactory, even if the doors and hot-plate covers are fixed and do not open. If you are a stickler for detail and want moving parts, there are plastic resin kits available for single, double and even fan-oven models (see page 30).

Materials

1 block of wood, or small, rigid box (suggested dimensions: 3½in (90mm) long, 2½in (65mm) high, 1¾in (45mm) deep)
Dressmaker's hooks and eyes, or similar
2 metal washers
2 domed metal screw covers from mirror fixing screws
Thick card or oddments or wood veneer
Gloss model enamel in one of the traditional Aga colours (white, dark green, red, cream or deep blue)
Black gloss model enamel
Aga logo and thermometer strip, cut from a magazine advertisement (optional)
Piece of thin metal rod (optional)

Building an Aga cooker

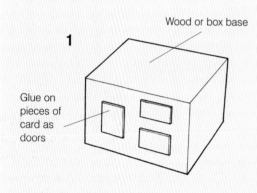

1

Wood or box base

Glue on pieces of card as doors

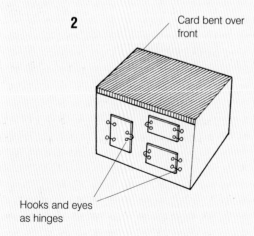

2

Card bent over front

Hooks and eyes as hinges

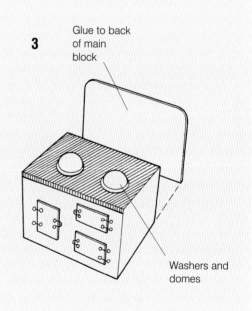

3 Glue to back of main block

Washers and domes

◀ When the Aga is painted, the surface resembles the enamel finish on a real Aga. Who could detect the humble materials it is made from?

Method

1　Cut three pieces of card for the doors and glue them in place on the front of the wood block (see photograph and diagram 1).

2　Glue the dressmaker's hooks and eyes to the doors to represent hinges and door catches. These will be painted over.

3　Undercoat the body of the Aga, and then topcoat in your chosen colour of model enamel.

4　Cut a piece of card the same length as the top of the wood block and ½in (12mm) deeper. Score the card and bend the excess ½in (12mm) downwards to form a lip over the front edge (see diagram 2). Paint it gloss black (including all the edges) and leave to dry, then glue to the top of the Aga.

5　Cut a second piece of card the same length as the back of the wood block, and about 1in (25mm) higher, curving the top corners as shown in diagram 3. This will form the back of the Aga. Paint gloss black and leave to dry, then glue in place. There is no need to paint the underneath of the card, but remember to paint the top and side edges, as they will show.

6　Glue the two washers to the top of the Aga and cover with the metal domes.

7　If you have managed to find an Aga logo and thermometer strip in a magazine, glue this in place on the front (see picture).

8　Another option is to add a metal rail along the front. For the Aga in the picture I used a metal fastening pin from an old brooch.

SCREENS

Screens are both decorative and useful, as they keep out draughts and can separate different areas of a room. In a dolls' house there is no need to worry about draughts, but a screen can make an attractive accessory. Here are methods for making two different types of screen.

CONCERTINA SCREEN

A concertina screen is simple and quick to make, and is a perfect way to use up an unwanted piece of 1/12-scale wallpaper or border pattern.

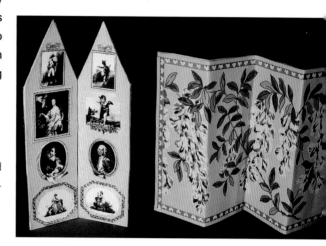

▲ An instant screen: the concertina screen can be made in 15 minutes. For the 'Gothick' screen on the left, I copied an idea from the 18th century and used some of the print room wallpaper design on a yellow paper – the favoured background colour of the time.

Method

1 Cut a rectangle from the card, approximately 8in (205mm) long and 5¼in (135mm) tall (or shorter if your room has limited space).

2 Cut out a matching rectangle of wallpaper and paste to the front of the card. Alternatively you could cut a smaller rectangle and surround this with a strip of border.

3 When the paste has dried out thoroughly, measure four equal sections on the card and score the back gently with a craft knife.

4 Fold the card into a concertina along the scored lines, pressing the sections together a few times to get the folds crisp and set in position.

Materials

Coloured or patterned card (about half the thickness of mounting board: gift boxes are a useful source)
Wallpaper or wallpaper border, to suit the room decor

HINGED SCREEN

This more sophisticated screen can also be plain and rectangular, but a rounded or pointed, 'Gothic' top on each panel adds interest and makes it suitable for a variety of interiors.

Method

1　First cut a paper pattern in your preferred style (see diagram 1 for suggestions). For a round-topped screen the panels should be 6in (150mm) tall at the top of the curve. The 'Gothick' screen should measure 6½in (160mm) at the point.

2　Fold the paper pattern in half lengthwise to check that any shaping is symmetrical and trim if necessary.

3　Using the paper pattern as a guide, cut out the required number of panels in the stiff card.

4　For a two-panel screen, make a tape hinge and glue to the back of the two panels as in diagram 2. For a three-panel screen, make a second tape hinge and glue to the front between the second and third panels.

5　Cut your chosen fabric or wallpaper to shape for each panel (again using the paper pattern) and glue to the front of the screen.

6　Cover the back of each panel with self-adhesive felt or plain paper. Dark green replicates the green baize traditionally used on the reverse (servants' side) of screens, or choose a simple fabric or paper to complement the pattern on the front.

7　Edge with braid if desired.

Materials

Stiff card (mounting board) or thin wood
Dressmaking tape or seam binding
Fabric or wallpaper to suit the surrounding decor
Self-adhesive felt (available in small sheets to attach to the base of ornaments or lamps), or thick plain paper or fabric, preferably dark green
Narrow decorative braid (optional)

Alternative patterns and construction for a hinged screen

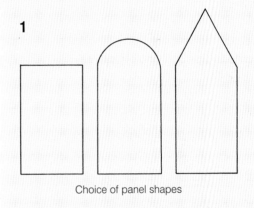

1

Choice of panel shapes

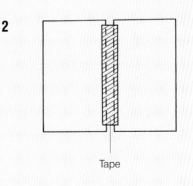

2

Tape

TRANSFORMING FURNITURE

An economical way to provide furniture for your dolls' house is to transform ready-made items with a paint finish. Imported furniture is widely available and generally cheap. The shapes and styles are often good, if sometimes lacking in delicacy. The finish, however, is usually unsatisfactory, generally because unsuitable high-gloss varnish has been used and applied too thickly. Do not let this deter you; pieces can easily be made far more attractive.

When using spray paint, cover the surrounding area with layers of newspaper, make sure there is good ventilation, and place the object inside a large cardboard box. Model suppliers sell spray paint designed for use on small surfaces; car spray paint is much too thick, and clogs delicate wire mesh and other small apertures. With each piece, the first step is to strip and clean all the surfaces.

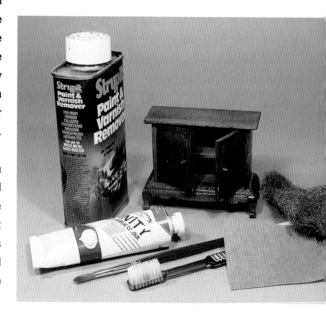

▲ Before work: a cupboard a stained with dark-coloured gloss varnish.

STRIPPING AND CLEANING

1   Cover your work table with layers of newspaper. Keep a piece of rag handy for any mopping up.

2   Apply paint-stripper following the instructions, using wire wool and an old toothbrush to work it into any carving or small corners. Keep a window open for ventilation and wear rubber gloves.

3   When the varnish is removed, wipe the piece over with white spirit and leave it near an open window until the fumes evaporate.

4   Smooth over gently with fine glasspaper, working in the direction of the grain, and wipe with a clean, smooth cloth to remove any dust. The piece is now ready to paint or stain.

> **Distressed finish**
> The wood used in such miniatures is often a dark colour. If you want a pale, distressed finish, apply plenty of slightly-diluted household bleach with a rag, wearing rubber gloves to protect your hands. Leave for about 10 minutes. Wipe off the residue and leave the piece to air dry. Finally, wipe over with a vinegar and water solution mixed about half-and-half, and leave it to dry thoroughly.

LONGCASE CLOCK

This is the first of three examples of furniture transformations, with 'before' and 'after' pictures showing the effects that can be achieved on inexpensive furniture. The original paper modern clock face would not have survived the use of paint-stripper, so after refurbishment it was replaced by one in a more suitable style

Method

1 Strip off and prepare the wood as detailed opposite.

2 Paint with one coat of matt green model enamel.

3 Leave until barely dry to the touch, then follow with a coat of bright green gloss enamel.

4 Wipe off patches of this second coat immediately with a cloth dipped in white spirit. This will tone down the green and leave some of the original wood colour showing through.

5 Glue on a new face and fit a small brass curtain ring as a surround. Suitable pictures of clock faces can be found in gift catalogues and magazine advertisements.

◄ Before: apart from its poor finish, this is a nicely-detailed longcase clock. The cresting on the top is a good feature and it even has a hanging brass pendulum inside, but the paper dial reproduces a modern clock face.

◄ After: a slightly-distressed finish was chosen for the clock, which can now be used as an antique.

TALL CUPBOARD WITH SHELVES

This adaptable cupboard was repainted in French blue model enamel for use in a kitchen. For a landing or a bedroom you might prefer a more discreet colour, perhaps pale blue or cream.

Method

1 Remove the plastic film from the door panels.

2 Strip off the varnish and smooth the wood both inside and out.

3 Paint the outside of the cupboard.

4 Line the door panels with mesh. Miniature wire mesh is available, or use the slightly stretchy plastic mesh found around some wine bottles (see photograph). Plastic mesh bags from chocolates, fruit or cheese are also suitable.

5 Make a paper pattern to fit the inside of the door and cut the mesh exactly to size.

6 Apply a minute trail of all-purpose glue to the inner edges of the door panels with a wooden cocktail stick. Leave until tacky and then press the mesh firmly into place.

7 If the cupboard is to be used for food, paint the inside pale blue, a colour thought to deter flies. To display crockery, the shelves can be lined with wallpaper in the traditional way.

▲ Before: the cupboard could be used to store china or linen so the contents will be on show.

► After: the cupboard's French blue finish makes it perfect for a kitchen. The plastic film over the doors has been replaced with mesh.

HARP

This harp was nicely-strung and even had brass foot pedals, but was varnished in an unpleasant red-brown colour that was meant to represent mahogany. A simple but effective transformation revealed its hidden beauty, rendering it fit to grace any music-room or high-class salon.

Method

1. Strip and prepare the piece as before, taking care to avoid damage to the stringing (paint stripper will not damage brass fittings).

2. Repaint with satin-finish black model enamel: use a size 00 brush on the inner edges to avoid smudging paint on to the strings.

3. Add gold decoration with a gold marker pen, shaking the pen vigorously before and during use. A pattern of random swirls is easy to achieve and will look impressive. The top and base of the harp can be covered with gold.

▲ Before: the harp's potential is hidden under thick varnish.

▶ After: the harp has been repainted black, with striking gold decoration added using a marker pen.

12
Decorative detail

Previous sections have shown basic techniques for decorating and furnishing your dolls' house. Here are some decorative ideas using a selection of items which are worth saving. It is amazing what can be done in a dolls' house scale with even the most everyday objects.

PAPER AND CARD

Paper and card are useful sources for imaginative effects for dolls' house interiors. It is worth salvaging anything you think looks interesting from packages, greetings cards and giftwrap. Advertising leaflets sometimes yield a tiny picture or an attractive border (see opposite – the border in the main room of my shop). Left-over wallpaper can be used to line shelves and drawers, or to make a screen (see page 124).

MARBLED PAPER

Marbled paper can be used instead of wallpaper (see page 104). It is also ideal for elegant fireplace panels and hearths (see opposite and page 80). It can be used to make covers for miniature books: simply glue round a small piece of wood. Shiny marbled paper can be made into a table top, or a floor if you have the right sort of house.

▶ Photographs of marble cut from glossy magazines and advertising leaflets. The black-and-white marble in the background is a photograph of a real marble surface, which I later used to make a floor.

▲ Blue-and-white tiles have many uses. Tile-design cards make decorative panels; wallpaper suits a kitchen or bathroom, and real ceramic tiles are the height of luxury for a grate surround. Shown are a greetings card, pictures from magazines, tile-patterned wallpaper and miniature ceramic tiles.

THE ORIENTAL LOOK

Gift wrap with an oriental theme makes perfect wallpaper for an 18th-century room. A Chinese-style picture from a magazine can be used as a wall panel, framed in a wooden moulding.

▶ This corner of the main room in my interior design shop is used to display classical furniture together with some Chinoiserie. The black-and-gold Chinese wall panels are framed in narrow stripwood, painted gold. The unusual surround above the fireplace was designed specially to show off the oriental painting of leopards on the mantelshelf.

PICTURES

A room without any pictures always seems unfinished. Look around, and I am sure you will see at least one picture on the wall, or perhaps a framed photograph or two on a table or desk. Pictures complete a room setting in the dolls' house too: gilt-framed paintings in a Victorian parlour, tiny silhouettes in oval frames in a Regency house, or a bold and colourful work in a wooden frame in a modern sitting room. Plan picture arrangements carefully to suit the style of decoration.

Once you have decided on the type of picture that will complement your scheme, look out for small reproductions that will catch the mood of the period. Magazines are an excellent source of suitably-sized pictures. The more expensive interior decoration magazine will have the best selection, as these are then printed on good-quality paper with the colouring exactly in register. Art and antiques periodicals will also offer a good yield.

▲ An art gallery is the perfect place to display a selection of miniature paintings. This one is lit to set off the paintings to perfection.

◀ Architectural prints hung over an elegant side table make an attractive group.

PHOTOCOPYING

Pen-and-ink sketches reduce well to the miniature scale, and provide some variety from the more usual coloured pictures. I used a photocopier to miniaturize several sketches for a house with a William Morris theme. Colour photocopies are now so good that, although they are unsuitable for reproducing oil paintings because the texture looks too smooth, watercolours and prints can be copied and scaled down very efffectively.

The picture will need to be reduced several times in order to scale it down to the size you want, and you may find it useful to reinforce detail or thicken some of the lines at an intermediate stage. Each time the size is reduced, the picture will become darker and less clear, as minute patches of shading will show up where lines have merged and spoil the effect. Conceal the unwanted marks with liquid paper, so that the end result is a miniature sketch that is clean and sharp. This takes a bit of patience, but makes a change from cutting every picture from magazines.

◀ This sketch by Edward Burne-Jones was miniaturized by using a photocopier and conveys all the charm and clarity of the original. It shows William Morris presenting an engagement ring to Janey, his wife-to-be.

◀ Regency fashion plates are sometimes shown on greeting cards and museum postcards. This elegantly dressed lady is one of a series.

FRAMING

Small pictures can be framed to good effect in gilt jewellery mounts, which are designed to hold cameos or stones. Fake cameos cost very little and can be used as intended. Gilded frames complete with replica carving are also available in toy shops that stock children's dolls' house furniture.

◀ Inexpensive gilt jewellery mounts are used to frame cameos and silhouettes. Fake Wedgwood plaques make effective fireplace inserts.

WOODEN FRAMES

To make your own wooden frames, you will need a metal mitre box and saw (see page 59) and 1/12-scale wooden picture frame mouldings. The mitred corners are cut in the same way as the fireplace mouldings (see page 79). Beware of dwarfing your picture with an outsize frame: framed pictures featured in magazines will give you an idea of the size of mouldings likely to be most suitable.

Method

1 Cut out your chosen picture and glue on to a piece of fine white card, allowing a wide border all round. Use all-purpose glue rather than paper glue, which could cause wrinkles.

2 Using a piece of wooden moulding as a guide, lay it in place along each side of the picture in turn and draw along it with a pencil to mark out on the card the finished dimensions of the frame. Trim the card to this size.

3 Cut the mouldings using the mitre box and saw. The opposite sides of the frame must be precisely the same length for a good fit. After cutting the first piece, mark the length for the second piece with a very sharp pencil before cutting. Repeat the process for the other two opposite sides.

4 Glue the mouldings around the picture on top of the spare card: smear each piece of moulding with all-purpose glue and leave until slightly tacky before fixing. This will avoid the danger of getting any glue on to the picture itself.

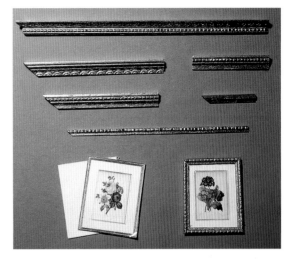

▲ Choose simple or ornate gilded picture frame mouldings to complement the style of painting to be framed.

Painted frames
Mahogany picture frame moulding needs no painting, but the edge of the backing card will need colouring to match, to avoid a white line showing. Use a felt-tip pen to colour the card neatly. If you prefer gilded picture frames, paint the card edges, and the strips of moulding before cutting, and touch up the corners if necessary after gluing the frame together.

▲ A Regency portrait of a mother with her son is appropriately framed in an embossed gilded moulding.

PICTURE-HANGING

The way pictures are hung will enhance their impact. One large painting, fixed with a small dot of adhesive putty at each corner, will look effective and imposing over a fireplace or in the centre of a wall. Take a tip from professional picture hangers and arrange smaller pictures in groups. Two or four prints of similar subjects hung close together give a better impression than assorted pictures spaced evenly around the room. The pictures also need to relate to any nearby furniture: try different arrangements, using a small blob of adhesive putty, until you find the layout you like best.

If the room has a fitted picture rail, suspend pictures from it with fine gilt string (glued to the rail and picture back). An alternative for a particularly ornate Victorian room is to attach a piece of thin brass rail to the wall with two eye-hooks screwed into the wall. Hang the pictures from two pieces of gilt string (see diagram). Glue beads on to each end of the rod as finials.

Small pictures in oval or round frames can be hung with a bow or thin velvet ribbon. A length of thin velvet ribbon with a bow at the top can also be used to suspend several small pictures in square or rectangular frames (see diagram).

Using a brass rail to hang pictures

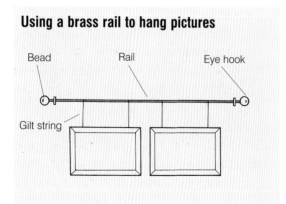

Suspending several pictures on a ribbon.

Decorating an oval frame with a bow.

TINY TOUCHES

It is well worth starting an oddments box of scraps of material, narrow ribbons, braids and lace trimmings, unusual beads or metal fastenings, and so on. A dolls' house owner never throws small items away. When you want to make an item, there is bound to be something in the oddments box which can be turned to miniature use.

My own bits box, which has evolved over many years, contains unusual buttons salvaged from long-gone clothing, wallpaper and fabric samples, gilt string and a pile of magazine cuttings with ideas I might want to adapt to small-size furnishing schemes. I keep old birthday and Christmas cards with small designs, and even envelopes if the lining is an unusual texture or colour. Here are some ideas for using ribbon, braid, lace, cord and other scraps. You will soon think of others once you are accustomed to looking at materials with 1/12-scale ideas in mind.

EMBROIDERED RIBBON

Thin, embroidered or patterned ribbon will make a decorative bell pull to hang by the fireplace in a drawing room. Attach the top to a small brass ring and mitre the bottom edge (fold and sew the bottom corners back to form a point). Sew a small bead on to the point to finish.

FURNISHING BRAID

Furnishing braid can make realistic stair carpet, as it is usually thick enough to look suitably sturdy, but malleable enough to be fitted right to the back of the treads. Attach with double-sided adhesive tape so that, if you want a change it can be removed easily.

Making a bow

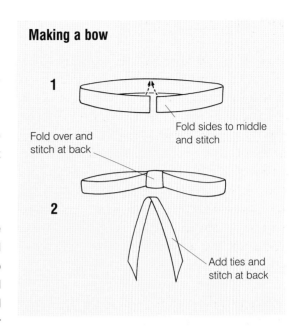

1 Fold over and stitch at back — Fold sides to middle and stitch

2 Add ties and stitch at back

RIBBON BOW

A small-scale bow must be made up, not tied, to make it neat and flat. This method should make a fiddly process simple.

Method

1 Cut a piece of ⅛in (3mm) wide ribbon about 2¼in (60mm) long. Fold in half, crease the fold, then fold in half again and crease the second fold. Using the creases as a guide, fold sides to middle and stitch in the centre (see diagram 1).

2 Cut a second piece of ribbon approximately ¾in (20mm) long. Fold over the centre of the bow and stitch at the back, folding in and overlapping one edge over the other (see diagram 2).

3 Cut a third piece of ribbon to length for the tie ends. Crease in the centre and stitch to the back of the bow (see diagram 2). Cut ends at a slant.

EDGINGS

Very thin silk cord can be used to edge covered chairs, cushions and curtains. Stitch it carefully and make sure it lies straight, or the effect will be spoiled. Piping cord can be used as an alternative to a plainer cornice in a bathroom or a seaside cottage. Lace is available in a huge range of widths and styles. The narrowest is suitable for dolls' clothing. Picot-edge lace can be used to make a cornice. Extra-wide lace can be used to make bedroom drapes.

BUTTONS

Buttons can be used for all sorts of things around the dolls' house. A plain wooden button with a slight indentation makes a plate for a Tudor household. A metal button with a coat of arms makes an effective ''By Appointment' sign for a shop. A lion mask metal button in verdigris finish is used as a wall ornament in my interior design shop. If you have a box of buttons, look in it for inspiration. If not, start collecting now.

CURTAIN RINGS

Small brass curtain rings come in handy as simple frames for round pictures. Back with card as for jewellery mounts and wooden frames (see page 132).

TOGGLES

Cut the shaped ends from a wooden duffel coat toggle to use as feet for a bed (see diagram). A bell-shaped plastic toggle with a hole in the top could make a lampshade for a (non working) ceiling light in a modern house (see diagram).

▲ An exquisite Ribbon and Roses design bell pull, worked on silk gauze (40 holes per inch), is one of a selection available as a kit for those capable of such fine work. It can also be supplied ready worked.

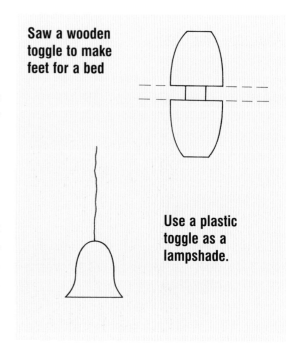

Saw a wooden toggle to make feet for a bed

Use a plastic toggle as a lampshade.

EARRINGS

Old clip earrings are just right for fastening back drapes or curtains in a grander room where simple ribbon or cord is not elaborate enough.

PLANT TIES

One of the easiest ways to make house plants is to use wired green plant ties. Trim the edges to a leaf shape and bend to make an aspidistra or fern.

SHELL ORNAMENTS

Tiny iridescent shells can be bought in packs; slightly larger specimens can be purchased separately. I have used shells in profusion in my interior design shop. They can be used in many ways. Single shells make good mantelshelf ornaments. Brightly coloured ones look beautiful heaped in little baskets or arranged in tiny gilt shells (available in craft shops).

▲ No self-respecting Victorian home would have been without an aspidistra. The jardinière is a suitable container for this easy to make plant.

Regency shell box

Regency ladies were found of covering boxes with patterns of shells, which were then varnished. I leave shells in their natural state as varnish darkens them.

▶ Use a small version of the real thing to create a decorative piece: these tiny shells appear identical in shape and colour to those twelve times the size.

Picture frame

Glue tiny shells on to a wooden picture frame or mirror surround, arranging them in a colourful pattern. If the shells are really small, it is easiest to pick them up with tweezers. Superglue is the best adhesive.

Shell tree

Another idea popular in the Regency period was making trees out of shells. You need a small glass dome on a wooden base (available in dolls' house shops). Glue a twig on to the wooden base. Sort your shells into colours that suggest flowers and glue in place on the twig, building up the design to resemble blossom. This is painstaking work but, if you have the patience, the result will be something special. The finished tree should fit neatly inside the glass dome.

BEADS

Like buttons, beads of all shapes and sizes can be put to good use in the dolls' house. Patterned macramé or unusual glass beads make perfect ornaments. A plain wooden bead can be transformed into a steamed pudding: tie in a piece of thin cotton or muslin and place in a saucepan on the stove.

Bead Tree

A large wooden bead can form the basis of a bay tree. If your house has no garden, stand bay trees in pots on either side of the front door, or use small ones as mantelshelf ornaments in a modern house.

Materials
1 large wooden bead
Pack of green flock powder (from model railway stockists)
PVA adhesive
Plastic wood filler
Twig or a wooden cocktail stick

▲ Topiary can be used indoors as well as outside. Miniature bay trees and a clipped yew can be made from wooden beads and a redundant chess piece.

Method

1   Fill the hole in the bead with wood filler. Push in the twig or stick to form the 'trunk'. Leave to set.

2   Brush paper glue on to the bead, hold by the 'trunk' and roll in the flock powder until well coated. You may need to repeat the process to cover it completely, but let the first coat set firmly first. If any bald patches remain after a second coat of glue and flock powder, drip on a little extra glue and press flock powder into the bald spot.

3   Fix the tree in a small pot with adhesive putty or wood filler. Glue on a layer of sesame seeds to represent pebbles.

CHESS PIECES

Old chess pieces are remarkably adaptable. If anyone in your family plays chess, they may have some spare pieces. Incomplete sets also turn up in charity shops, so it is worth looking out for them. They vary enormously in style, but the shapes shown are the most common. Variations may also be suitable for most uses. The base of any piece will make feet for a bed, stool or cupboard.

To make the accessories shown, the pieces must be sawn off at strategic places. The best way to hold a piece steady while cutting is to use a mitre box and fix the piece in place with a large lump of adhesive putty to keep it horizontal.

Pawns

The tops of pawns (see diagram) make excellent finials for newel posts or small gates.

Knights

Paint knights in a stone colour and use on either side of an imposing front door, or as gate piers for a large dolls' house. Black knights can be used as finials for newel posts on Tudor or Jacobean staircases.

Saw off the top of the piece and use the body as a base for a topiary tree (see diagram) using the same flock powder method as for the bay trees (see opposite). These formalised trees can be used in the dolls' house garden or indoors.

Bishops, Kings and Queens

The lower part of a king or queen will also make an attractively shaped urn (see photograph), which can be transformed with a painted verdigris finish or marbled effect (see page 107). A black piece could be left in its unpainted state to represent exotic ebony.

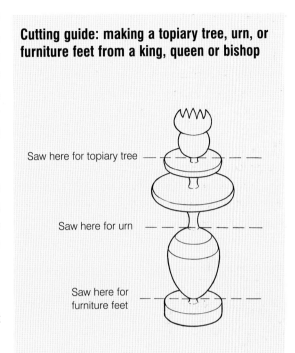

Cutting guide: making a topiary tree, urn, or furniture feet from a king, queen or bishop

Saw here for topiary tree

Saw here for urn

Saw here for furniture feet

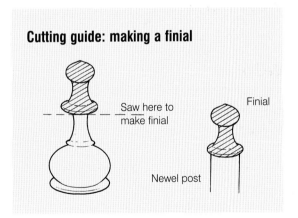

Cutting guide: making a finial

Saw here to make finial

Finial

Newel post

13
Practical gardening

Dolls' houses can be extended by the addition of a garden, and miniature gardening has distinct advantages over the real thing. You need not go out in the cold and get wet and muddy, but can garden in comfort on the dullest day. Climate and soil quality do not matter either. If you have sufficient space, a garden, whether large or small, is a definite asset for a dolls' house. This section offers practical tips and techniques for bringing your planned garden into being.

A BASIC GARDEN

When you have decided on the layout of your garden or patio and its principal features, make a plan on paper, or you could end up with too much crammed in, or some awkward gaps. Do not try to include too many features in a small space, or the result will be confused rather than restful. When you are satisfied with your plan, and know what you want, visit a model railway stockist for some scenic materials.

Materials
A piece of 'lawn' grass – sold in a roll or by the piece Packs of coloured flock powder for earth, sand and gravel, plus green to make hedges Foliage in a variety of colours Stiff cardboard Base board

Method

1. Cut out a piece of cardboard to use as a base. This will be fixed on top of the base board with double-sided tape, so can be replaced easily at a later stage if you decide on any changes. Copy your plan on to the card for accurate guidance.

2. Cut out the lawns and try the pieces of 'grass' for size, working from your plan. Set them aside, to be glued in after the paths and borders have been laid, to avoid sprinkling them with flock powder.

3. Brush PVA adhesive over the surfaces you have marked out as paths and sprinkle with sand or gravel flock powder. When the glue is dry, turn the card upside-down over a sheet of newspaper and tap it a few times to shake off the surplus. Repeat the process to cover any bald patches.

4. Make the borders and flowerbeds with earth flock powder in the same way. They will look better if you glue in an extra layer of thick card or scrunched-up paper first to raise them slightly.

5. Glue on the pieces of lawn.

▼ An espaliered tree against a brick wall is a space-saving idea in a tiny garden. A deckchair on the lawn completes the summery scene.

◀ The Orangery (opposite) is designed to fit against a house wall and has the useful feature of glazing fitted between the wooden panels so that it can be removed for painting or staining the wood. It is shown here with a kit garden made by the same manufacturer.

Terraces and paved paths

Paving is an alternative to sand or gravel paths. Sheets of 1/12-scale paving can be cut to fit your design (see page 88), or you can make your own paving stones from stone-coloured modelling compound. Purchased flagstones in resin or ceramic are a further option for a terrace, although more expensive (see page 97).

Trees

To make a natural-looking tree, use a twig as a trunk and glue on foliage, which is available in various shapes and sizes from model railway stockists. The foliage can be trimmed to any shape. If you want a more formal clipped tree, perhaps for a terrace or patio, follow the instructions for making an ornamental bay tree on page 138.

Hedges

For a neatly-trimmed hedge, use a strip of balsawood, about 1½ to 2in (40 to 50mm) thick, cut to height. Gently curve the top edge with a craft knife, spread it with glue and sprinkle thoroughly with green flock powder. Tap off the surplus powder when the glue has dried, and re-apply if necessary to cover any bald patches.

Creeper

A low wall on at least one side of the garden will make an excellent base for creeper. Make the wall from a strip of wood the height you want, and cover with stone or brick cladding. Foliage, as for trees, can be cut to shape and glued in place up the wall.

Flowers

Fill the borders and flowerbeds with colourful miniature flowers. I like to use a few choice specimens made by specialist craftspeople and make the rest myself from modelling compound. Dried flowers also look effective, but will need changing frequently as they fade. If you spray them with hair lacquer after arranging, they will last longer.

Pond

Use fake mirror glass (see page 145) to represent the water for a garden pond. Build up the edges into a raised bank by gluing on layers of paper or card, well covered with earth or grass flock powder, and arrange plants round the edges to disguise the join. Tiny real pebbles or 'rocks' (pieces of polystyrene packaging material, suitably painted) will also contribute to the attractiveness of a pond. Fix 'rocks' with polystyrene cement as all other glues will dissolve this material.

▶ This mini-greenhouse has become an Edwardian conservatory, the ideal spot to spend a lazy summer afternoon. I found the token garden roller in the corner on a junk stall: it is made of copper and brass.

GARDEN BUILDINGS

A garden building is an attractive addition to your miniature garden or patio and need not be expensive. You can make a greenhouse at very little cost, but if you are keen to add a superior conservatory, be prepared to pay rather more.

Conservatories are available in all shapes and sizes, and can become the centrepiece of a garden setting. There are some very grand models available, which can add a spectacular extra dimension to your dolls' house. You can buy ready made, as a kit, or even adapt a mini-greenhouse intended for seed propagation. These are not as realistic as a genuine miniature as there is no door and the roof simply lifts off. They are, however, an easy and inexpensive way to begin: you can always 'upgrade' the structure later.

When painting woodwork, use masking tape over any ready-fitted glass. I painted the Edwardian model opposite white. The floor is wrapping paper in a Pugin-style design, pasted down and covered with a thin sheet of acetate so it looks like shiny tiles. I fixed frilly metal roof-ridging on with superglue, added a miniature garden table and chair, and some plants. I have since added a trailing vine with tiny grapes, inside the roof.

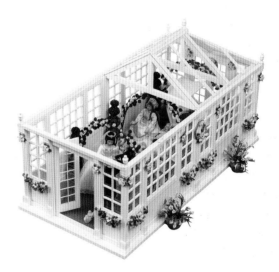

▶ Two Victorian conservatories joined together make a delightful venue for a wedding. This model is available as a kit or ready-built.

WINDOW BOXES

If you do not have enough space to create a miniature garden or terrace, why not add a touch of colour by putting window boxes on the house itself? Alternatively, these little boxes can be fixed at ground level to represent a flower border (see page 152).

Method

1 Cut two pieces of stripwood to the length required (e.g. to fit the length of the window).

2 Cut two more pieces approximately ½ to ¾in (12 to 20mm) long to from the ends of the box.

3 Glue together, taking care to fit the sides between the front and back lengths to make a neat front edge.

4 Paint the box white or green.

5 Fill with artificial flowers and leaves.

6 Attach the boxes to the front of the house with adhesive putty rather than fixing them in place permanently. This will make it easier to change the flower arrangement later if wanted.

Materials

Thin stripwood about ½in (12mm) wide
White or green paint
Artificial flowers and/or foliage

▲ A window box along the front of this little shop is filled with artificial flowers (of the sort normally used to trim hats).

JAPANESE GARDEN

Japanese gardens have a special tranquillity which appeals to many Westerners. I made a small one for myself on a balcony, and was so delighted with the result that I planned an even smaller version for a dolls' house. My son adapted and extended my design to make a setting for a tiny garden pavilion.

Materials

Flat wooden box with a raised edge – I used a box that had contained soap measuring 6¾ x 8½in (170 x 215mm)
Piece of emery paper, grade 2
Small black, white and grey pebbles
Small pagoda or oriental-looking ornament (you may find a decoration sold for a tropical fish tanks suitable)
Plastic plants intended for use in fish tanks
Plasticine
Green flock powder
Fake mirror glass (optional)

▶ This peaceful garden is the perfect setting for an oriental building. Real evergreen foliage adds to the natural effect, but will need replacing occasionally. An alternative is a tree made from a gnarled twig, with fake foliage glued on.

Method

1 Cut the emery paper to fit inside the box. Leave it in its natural state for golden sand, but if you prefer grey-white sand, paint it with very pale grey emulsion. Either is suitable for this type of garden.

2 Place shrubs and pebbles strategically, singly or in groups of odd numbers, such as three or five. A traditional garden designed for contemplation needs only a few, and in a true Japanese garden, groups of even numbers are considered unlucky.

3 Cut the plastic water plants to the shapes you want and embed in a little mound of Plasticine. Brush the Plasticine with PVA adhesive and cover with green flock powder to represent moss.

4 A more elaborate garden can have additional features. Fix an ornament in Plasticine or make a small pond from fake mirror glass, disguising edges with moss or small shrubs.

5 For a natural scenic effect, arrange a pile of stones in one corner.

6 A simple bridge over a pond can be made from several thin strips of wood, stained and glued with a very thin strip as a handrail.

TINY GARDENS

For the smaller house, an ideal place for a tiny garden or patio is at the side of the house. All you need to do is add a base board of a size to suit your ideas. It is best to use a piece of sturdy blockboard about ⅝in (16mm) thick. Blockboard made of MDF is available from timber merchants or home decoration stores. If you plan to attach a lean-to conservatory to the house, the base board will need to be secured firmly. Use two large hinges or, if available, strips of metal drilled for screws, and fix these to the base of the house and the base of the blockboard, where they will not show. If you do not plan to attach anything more than creeper to the house, the board can just be butted against the house wall.

If this is your first attempt at creating a dolls' house garden, you can start with a simple design and develop it into something more ambitious later on. If possible, allow extra space for 'growth' right from the start.

▲ A neat patio outside the front door gives a `fresh-air' feel, even if there is no space for a proper garden.

INTERNAL COURTYARD

In a larger period property another option is to use one room to arrange a garden courtyard inside the house. This idea was suggested by many courtyard gardens seen down passageways or through entrance gates in the Cotswolds, where an internal courtyard filled with flowers is a common feature.

◄ Flagstones are essential for an effective garden courtyard. Plaster or 'cast-iron' resin wall plaques add to the outdoor feeling. Plants in pots and tubs or on a pedestal can be moved round to suit your mood or the season, for a changing scene to give lasting pleasure.

PERIOD GARDENS

However small your garden or patio, the secret of success is good planning. Design it on paper first, making sure that you can fit all the features you want in the space available. If you have a period-style house its garden can complement it perfectly. Here are a few suggestions:

▲ Statuary and urns are particularly effective in a garden. These realistic examples were carved from wood, then covered with plaster and painted to reproduce the effect of weathered stone and add an air of grandeur.

TUDOR HERB GARDEN

Design a Tudor or Jacobean-style knot garden, with beds of flowers and herbs arranged in a formal pattern. Arrange earth or paved paths between beds.

GEORGIAN FORMAL GARDEN

Square or rectangular beds of flowers can be divided by gravel paths. Neatly-trimmed low hedges should surround the flower beds, with small standard trees placed at regular intervals.

VICTORIAN FLOWER GARDEN

A piece of sculpture makes a good centrepiece, and you can use a wedding-cake pillar as a pediment for a statue or urn. Surround with plenty of colourful flowers, paved or grassed in between the beds.

▲ A wedding-cake pillar gives height to this arrangement of exquisite flowers.

COTTAGE GARDEN

A winding path can be created from miniature bricks or paving made from modelling compound, with fake moss glued into the cracks. A miniature stone sink makes a good container for fake or dried plants and flowering creeper.

ACCESSORIES

To add life to the scene, it is fun to give the impression that some activity has been going on in the dolls' house garden. A watering can and mini-trowel or garden fork can be left ready for use, together with a few plant pots and some packets of seeds. Seed packets can be made simply by folding small pieces of paper into envelopes and writing the plant name clearly using a fine-line pen. A coiled green shoelace with a metal end makes an effective garden hose.

▲ The maker adapted full-size plans in a book of American country patterns from the nineteenth century to produce this delightful octagonal gazebo.

◀ A miniature wheel-barrow and other tools can bring a garden scene to life.

▼ This attractive conservatory is easy to put together from a ready-painted kit with glazed panels fitted. Here it is the centrepiece in a garden that is also available as a kit to fit neatly against a dolls' house wall.

UPKEEP

A miniature garden needs a certain amount of maintenance – to keep dust rather than weeds at bay. Go over it occasionally using a small feather to flick off dust, and if necessary use a moist cotton bud and a small piece of damp cloth.

If you include dried flowers rather than plastic ones you will need to replace them occasionally to keep the garden looking fresh and colourful. There is nothing worse than plants that look dead.

▲ ▼ No serious gardener could manage without a shed where tools can be stored when not in use. This model has a lift-off roof, so that it is easy to arrange plants and flowers as well as all the tools. It has a large window on each side so that everything can be seen clearly when the roof has been put back on.

14

Renovation

Interest in old dolls' houses has increased with the growth of the hobby. This is often the starting point for someone who still has the house with which they or their children played. The idea of renovating an old favourite can be tempting, but there are a few points to consider first.

A dolls' house which has been handed down through more than one generation in a family may be a genuine treasure, and it is wise to check when it was made. Consult your local museum curator or a dolls' house magazine for an opinion: provide a photograph in the first instance. Another point to consider is whether the house is a candidate for conservation, restoration, or renovation, as each option will require a different level of work. A beautifully-made Victorian or Edwardian house which has been neglected would still be appreciated enormously by a collector, and would lose much of its value if radically altered. Collectors enjoy houses with the original wallpapers and paintwork, even though these may be in poor condition. Such a house would simply need careful cleaning, preferably by an expert. Restoring a rickety old house demands considerable time and patience, and you may find that starting again from scratch will be more satisfying. If the house is not of sentimental value, why not put your small property on the market, buy a new dolls' house with the proceeds, and make a fresh start? .

If you have some decorative ideas you would like to try out before beginning on a new dolls' house, an old house could provide a useful practice ground. An old home-made house is another candidate for restoration, and here you need to take a close look and ask yourself, 'Is it really worth it?' If the house is badly made from poor quality wood, or infected with woodworm, and the architectural style is of no known provenance, however much care and attention you lavish on updating it, you will probably remain unsatisfied with the results. Again, it might be better to channel your energies into new work.

▲ The original plain, roughly finished house with a poor roof was a candidate for complete renovation. With the addition of wooden mouldings, a solid-looking door stained dark oak, and a roof covering of thick hessian to represent thatch, it became a Tudor character residence.

The type of house most commonly available for renovation is by Tri-ang, or one of its contemporaries. Various brands of commercially-made dolls' houses were produced in large numbers from the 1920s to the 1960s, all made in 1⁄16 scale. They have a nostalgic charm, particularly for anyone who played with one as a child. More often than not, the original wallpaper will be in tatters and too far gone to keep.

I prefer to restore this type of house to something approaching its original appearance so that it can be enjoyed by a new generation of children. If you prefer the faded, period look, then all you can do is to clean the house thoroughly and leave well alone.

▲ Brick paper covers a multitude of faults on this old, obviously home-made house. The door was replaced and framed with mouldings, and lanterns and boot-scrapers added to liven up the large expanse of brick.

CLEANING BEFORE REDECORATION

Method

1 Give the house a careful scrub from top to bottom. Watch out for any nails left sticking up. This is a messy job, so work outdoors if possible. Remove old wallpaper by wetting it thoroughly: leave for a few minutes and use a scraper. Leave the house to dry in the open air or by a window.

2 Traces left by carpeting that has been glued firmly in place can be difficult to remove. Although the carpet can be pulled away fairly easily, it may leave a sticky residue on the floor. If hot water alone does not work, try different solvents on small patches until you find one that makes an impression. It will be a matter of trial and error and guesswork. White spirit often works well. If the glue really will not come off, it will simply have to be covered up with a new covering – or you may be able to sandpaper the marks away.

3 Sometimes an old house will have been painted in unsuitable colours with gloss paint, itself an inappropriate finish. Use a proprietary brand of paint-stripper and wire wool, in a well-ventilated room or, preferably, outdoors. Always wear rubber gloves when using paint-stripper, and cover surrounding surfaces.

4 Rub over with glasspaper until the surface is smooth and wipe it over with white spirit to leave a really clean surface for redecoration.

POINTS TO WATCH

An old and neglected dolls' house is bound to need some repairs before it can be redecorated. Here are some of the most common problems, and how to deal with them. Once put in order, a decorative scheme in keeping with the original appearance will give the best effect. When you restore an old dolls' house, it is nice to think that the old owner might recognise it.

ROOFS

The roofs on most Tri-ang era houses were made of thick cardboard, layered firmly together and coloured red. The corners were very vulnerable and you may find that the layers have separated and some of the cardboard is missing. The simplest approach is to cut new sections of similar-weight cardboard and fit and glue them in to make the corners up to the right thickness. Try to match the original roof colour by mixing acrylic paint.

▲ This flat-roofed Tri-ang house is neat and trim after renovation. The metal sliding front now moves easily and the ledge at the base provides a small space for a few flowering plants.

METAL SLIDING FRONTS

Some Tri-ang houses had sliding metal fronts, which may have become battered over the years. If you have one, try to straighten out the bent metal as much as possible. The metal is quite soft, so do not use a hammer because it may do more harm than good. Careful and patient bending by hand is the best method. Make sure that the front runs smoothly in the grooves at the top and bottom. Clean the grooves carefully, then use a candle to wax the runners until the front slides easily to open and close.

DOOR AND WINDOWS

Tri-ang, Romside and Gee Bees houses all had metal front doors and windows with lattice panes. These were also sold separately for the dolls' house builder. It is still possible to obtain replacement doors and windows in the correct scale from some hobby shops and mail order outlets, although they will now be made of plastic, not metal. For a home-made house you will probably need to custom-build a wooden door to fit the doorway.

PAINTED EXTERIORS

Most Tri-ang houses had flowers painted directly on to the front walls to provide a token garden – hollyhocks were the most favoured species. When renovated, a plain house can be enhanced by something similar, if your painting skills are good enough. A window box or two, or some flowers or creeper around the front door would also be a simple way of livening up the front in a fresh way (see page 144).

THE INTERIOR

If you have taken the trouble to renovate an old dolls' house, you probably have firm ideas on how you want the interior to look. Alternatively, if you are more interested in conservation and restoration and want to keep the period look of, say, a 1930s Tri-ang house, it is worth bearing in mind the preferred colour schemes of the day. The wealth of interior decoration ideas and possibilities available today simply did not exist, and many houses tended to be uniform inside (see page 25 for ideas on colour schemes).

FURNITURE

It is not easy to find furniture in the correct 1/16 scale to suit these older houses, but occasionally pieces turn up in antique markets and at some miniatures fairs, where old as well as new pieces are included. Professional miniaturists make replicas of furniture in various sizes and, if you choose carefully, you may be able to find some which will be of a reasonable size for your house. If you make some of the things I have suggested, remember to scale them down slightly.

▼ The roof and window frames of this Gee Bees house needed attention when it was bought in a street market, but it was otherwise in reasonable condition. Cream paint for the windows is a more pleasing contrast with the blue than the original bright yellow, and new glazing is a great improvement. The windows now open easily and after repair, which included fitting a new roof ridge (see page 74), the roof was repainted with acrylic paint.

16
Further reading

So much useful reference material is available, covering both dolls' and real houses as well as furnishings, interior design and gardens that it is impossible to list them all. You may find this small selection interesting:

PERCIVAL, Joyce, Architecture for Dolls' Houses GMC Publications, 1996

STEWART-WILSON, Mary, Queen Mary's Dolls' House, The Bodley Head, 1988

STEWART-WILSON, Mary, Miniature Rooms: The Thorne Rooms at the Art Institute of Chicago, The Art Institute of Chicago and Abbeville Press NY

GRANGER, Janet, Needlepoint Carpets, GMC Publications, 1996

SCARR, Angie, Making Miniature Food and Market Stalls, GMC Publications, 2001

LIST OF SUPPLIERS

Anglesey Dolls' Houses
Telephone: + 44 (0) 1407 763511
Fax: +44 (0) 1407 763511
www.angleseydollshouses.co.uk

Borcraft Miniatures
www.borcraft-miniatures.co.uk

Dolls' House Workshop
Telephone: +44 (0) 870 757 2372
Fax: +44 ()) 870 757 2375
www.dollshouseworkshop.com
(Colour catalogue available)

Elphin Dollshouses
www.ElphinDollshouses.co.uk

Jeremy Collins
(Gable End Designs)
www.gable-end-designs.co.uk

The Dolls' House Emporium
Freephone: 0800 0523 643
Fax: +44 (0) 1773 513772
Overseas orders (including
Channel Islands and Eire):
Telephone:+44 (0) 1773 514424
www.dollshouse.com
(Free colour catalogue)
Glenowen Ltd
Telephone: +44 (0) 116 240 4373
www.glenowendhf.co.uk

Margaret's Miniatures
Telephone: +44 (0) 1985 846797
Fax: +44 (0) 1985 846796

Caroline Nevill Miniatures
Telephone/Fax
+44 (0) 1225 443091
www.carolinenevillminiatures.co.uk

Sid Cooke Dolls' Houses
Telephone: +44 (0) 1922 633422
www.sidcooke.com
(Colour catalogue available)

ACKNOWLEDGEMENTS

I would like to thank Gerrie Purcell for initiating this revised and expanded edition of my best-selling book, and for her unstinting help when I needed advice. Thanks are due to my editor Alison Howard who dealt so competently with the organization of so many new pictures and additional text.

A big thank you to my husband, Alec, for so uncomplainingly taking new photographs, which are sure to provide extra inspiration for readers. I also want to thank my friend June Wright, whose enthusiasm for dolls' houses and interest in this project sparked off new ideas for me to work on. I am grateful to Margaret's Miniatures of Warminster and Caroline Nevill Miniatures of Bath who generously loaned miniatures for our photography. And finally, thanks to all the makers who kindly loaned pictures or allowed us to photograph their work:

Wendy Allin (shell tray, 137). Anglesey Dolls' Houses (Gamekeeper's Cottage, 12; Victoria House, 19; Gothic folly, 63; Tudor table and benches kit, 119). David Booth (Regency chaise longue, 34). Borcraft Miniatures (room box with Christmas scene, 54; period-style wooden mouldings, 92; Victorian kitchen furniture kits, 121; gilded mouldings, 133). Christopher Cole (small-scale Georgian house, 10; green Georgian shop, 71 and 144). Dolls' House Workshop (Willow Cottage, 15; Jubilee Terrace with flower shop, 46; Primrose Cottage, 51; Vine House, 51; Jubilee Terrace house, 13). Judith Dunger, (Lacover table, 35). ELF (country house bathroom fitment, 38); Elphin Dollshouses (1930s semi-detached house, 16). Farthingale (stone garden urns, 147); Gable End designs (four-oven Aga cooker, 30). Glenowen Ltd. (Moormead ready-painted house, 14). Honeychurch Toys Ltd. (Wealden House, 8, 67 and 70; 18th-century shop, 64). Lenham Pottery (modern shower fitment, 39). Robert Longstaff Workshops (Lutyes-style garden bench kit, 118). Sid Cooke Dolls' Houses (Silver Jubilee House, 15, 17 and 18; porch, 18; Orangery Garden, 140). John Watkins (early Victorian House, 9 and 19); Merry Gourmet Miniatures (food and flowers, 30; Georgian food, 36; patio courtyard, 146; garden setting with deckchair, 141; flower arrangements, 147; wheelbarrow with tools and vegetables, 148). The Dolls' House Emporium (Fern Villa interior, 26; conservatory and garden kit, 148; Camellia Cottage, 50; Oak Hurst, 53; Cumberland Castle and East Wing, 53; Pembroke Grange, 69; Mill Cottage, 75; Cadogan Gardens doorway, 77; Victorian double conservatory, 143). Nicola Mascall (needlepoint bell pull, 136). Mini Mundus (Biedermeyer sofa kit, 121). Guy Nisbett (Japanese Garden 145). C&Y Roberson (metal bedstead, 31; Regency shower, 38; metal chair, 38; metal cradle, 114; 1880s bassinet perambulator, 45; Harry Saunders (brick chimney with lead flashing, 75). Stokesay Ware (jardinière 137). Sussex Crafts (Adam-style fire surround, 33 and 78; flagstones, 101). Keith Thorne (gazebo, 148; Georgian doorway and railings, 71. Bernardo Traettino (Adam-style window, 70).

PHOTOGRAPHIC ACKNOWLEDGEMENTS

Guild of Master Craftsman Publications gratefully acknowledges the following people and agencies for granting permission to reproduce their photographs in this book. The photographs on the following pages were supplied courtesy of:

Anglesey Dolls' Houses: 19; Borcraft Miniatures: 54 (bottom); Dolls' House Workshop: 13, 15 (bottom), 46, 51 (top and bottom); Elphin Dollshouses: 16; Gable End Designs: 30; Glenowen Ltd.: 14; Keith Thorne: 148 (top); The Dolls' House Emporium: 26, 50, 53 (top and bottom), 69, 75 (top), 77 (right), 143, 148 (bottom); Sid Cooke Dolls' Houses: 15 (top), 17–18 (photo by Berkshire Dolls' Houses), 140.

Index

ABOUT THE AUTHOR

Jean Nisbett began to take notice of period houses, their decoration and furniture before she was ten years old, and they have been a consuming passion ever since. While bringing up a family she began working in miniature scale, and has since developed an equal enthusiasm for reproducing modern architecture and design small scale. Her work has been shown on BBC televison, Channel 4, UK Style and TF1 France.

Jean began writing while working in the London offices of an American advertising agency, and she is well known as the leading British writer on dolls' houses and miniatures. Her articles have appeared in specialist dolls' house magazines since 1985, and regularly in GMC's *The Dolls' House Magazine* since the first issue in 1998. This is her ninth book for GMC Publications. She lives in Bath, Somerset.

Imperial and metric

The standard dolls' house scale is 1/12, which was based originally on imperial measures: one inch represents one foot. Although many craftspeople use metric measurements, dolls' house hobbyists in Britain and especially in America still use feet and inches. In this book imperial measures of length are given first, followed by their metric equivalent. Accuracy to the millimetre is generally unnecessary, and metric measurements may be rounded up or down a little. Practically all the miniatures in this book are to 1/12 scale.